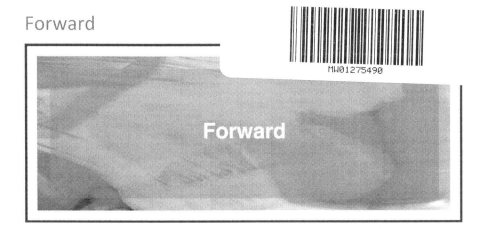

Ready to discover how to work and play better with others so they seek you out? More than ever, these times call for us to know exactly how.

Why? In our increasingly connected world, evil and good actions hit faster, from more places, and can spread farther. And more people are living and working alone.

Your key to success you can savor in all parts of your life is your capacity to connect in more situations around sweet spots of mutual interest.

That's your straightest path to leveraging serendipitous events and friendships to evoke smarter mutual support sooner, and capture more opportunities.

More than your money, title, attractiveness, charisma or even your strongest talent, your capacity to create mutuality enables you to become *the* Opportunity Maker with whom others most want to align.

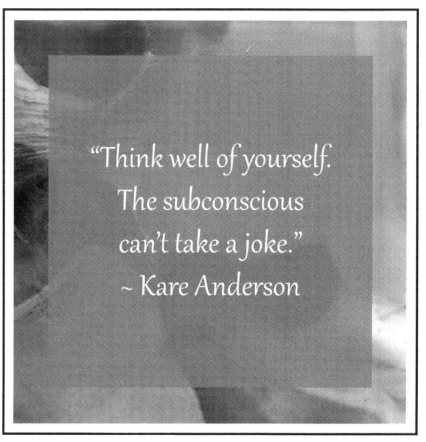

"Think well of yourself.
The subconscious
can't take a joke."
~ Kare Anderson

As an Emmy-winning former NBC and *Wall Street Journal* reporter, I've spent the past decade translating behavioral research into practical ways that you can become more widely quoted as you become more deeply connected.

On this path of learning, you can discover how to involve unexpected allies, provide them with bragging rights, create self-organized teams, and become a trusted subject matter expert for your key media. As well you can learn ways to co-create the situations, products, services and programs that scale opportunity for all participants. That's how you become consistently sought-after.

In a world where The Law of Unexpected Consequences is becoming the norm, your mutuality mindset can keep you attract opportunities, via apt alliances, rather than being pulled under by forces over which you have no control.

*Mutuality makes
a greater
you and me*

Ready to turn the page to the adventure story you're truly meant to live?

Why Re-Set Your Life Towards a Mutuality Mindset?

Who Are You Becoming?

After winning several music awards one year, Carlos Santana was asked by an eager young entertainment reporter, how he felt about "this belated recognition after so many years as a professional musician." In an apparent *non sequitur*, Santana smiled warmly and replied, "I am becoming the people I love," to which the reporter responded, "But what does that have to do with the awards?" Santana explained, "To a greater degree over time, these friends, musical or not, seem to infuse my music and my life. And my friends say the same has happening to them." Then, looking gently at the reporter, Santana asked, "Have you had that gratifying feeling of mutuality?"

Hint: Becoming ever more deeply connected with those you admire and love bolsters, in you, the traits you most admire in them.

With whom do you spend the most time these days?

Have those shared experiences enabled you to:
- Do what you are most passionate about more often?
- Use your best talents with others who are too?
- Be sought-after by those who appreciate your passions and talents?
- Enjoy a life that's adventuresome, accomplished and meaningful?
- Feel a gratifying sense of friendship and belonging?

Would they say the same about being with you?

In our increasingly complex, yet connected world, those who cultivate a mutuality mindset are the lucky ones most likely to succeed and savor their lives with others.

Remember the many compartments of the heart, the seed of what is possible. So much of who we are is defined by the places we hold for each other. For it is not our ingenuity that sets us apart, but our capacity for love, the possibility our way will be lit by grace. Our hearts prisms, chiseling out the colors of pure light

Tip: Whatever most captures your attention most controls your life.

Ready to redefine your life around mutuality?

Though I still sometimes stumble on this path toward living a mutuality mindset, it remains my core belief. It is the single most nourishing, life-changing behavior I've found. Looking back on life so far, aren't your most positively indelible memories those where you accomplished something remarkable with others?

If Even I Can Find a Way to Mutuality, You Surely Can

Why do I believe this? Growing up I was a stutterer, once diagnosed as "phobically shy" yet I was simply trying to why people did what they did. Feeling an odd duck, I could not only not figure out how make conversation, let alone make friends. Over time, I've come to realize that many others, perhaps you too, have an insatiable desire to really connect, yet hesitant as to exactly how.

I may have become a journalist because it gave me the perfect excuse to ask questions. In so doing, I discovered how most people really want to tell their story. From thousands of interviews as a reporter for *The Sacramento Bee*, then the *Wall Street Journal,* and finally for NBC, I realized how often those I interviewed had trouble hearing the questions I asked, as they were so preoccupied with what they wanted to get across. Some didn't even investigate in advance or ask about the kind of stories I covered. In brief, few bothered to consider, in advance, what would be the best story to give me that matched the kind of stories I was hired to cover – and would further their goals.

Why Might You Move Toward a Mutuality Mindset?

One of our biggest mistakes we make is attempting to make others like us. Counter-intuitively, it's not *how* others feel about you that matters most. Rather *it is if they feel about themselves when around you*. If they like how they feel, they are inclined to like you. In fact they will often project onto you the qualities they most admire in others even, sometimes, if you have not demonstrated that you actually have those traits.

Conversely, if they don't like how they feel when around you, they will see the qualities in you they most dislike in others – even if you have not demonstrated those. Guess which feelings are felt most intensely and last longer? That's why an early step toward mutuality is bringing out the side they most like in themselves.

And there's always a sweet spot of shared interest, even among those with very different beliefs and goals, yet we can only discover it, to our mutual interest, if we are willing to look for it together. Understanding this point alone is life-changing. See how politics, religion, national pride, alone cause so many arguments and violence because neither "side" is willing to persist in bringing out the better side in the other and seeking that common ground. The same right/wrong inclination is the top killer of marriages and any kind of relationship.

"To be successful
you can't show up
to the potluck
with just a fork."
~ Dave Liniger

Take Three Steps Toward Greater Mutuality with Others

One: Deepen self-knowledge, to project less on others and thus be able to more clearly…

Two: Cultivate an empathic capacity and desire to step into their shoes, because only then can you speak to their interests first so they feel heard and motivate to respond.

Three: Explore and suggest sweet spots of shared interest, listening closely for another's response, to involve the other person in find those sweet spots.

Tip: "Many ideas grow better when transplanted into another mind than in the one where they sprung up." ~ Oliver Wendell Holmes

Be Quoted in the Next Edition of This Book?

I'd like to feature your specific mutuality-mindset-related tip and example – or one you've learned from someone else, properly attributed – in my next edition of this book. Please send it to me at kare@sayitbetter.com, in 200 words or less, with links, your full name, email address and your main URL. Together we can generate more value and visibility with and for others.

What Behavior Do You Feed?

A battle is going on between two wolves inside of you, the evil one and the good one, a Cherokee parable suggests. Which trait wins, in how you behave with others, especially when under stress? The one you feed (practice) the most, of course. Hear how to keep feeding your good wolf in podcasts from Oliver Burkeman, author of *The Antidote: Happiness for People Who Can't Stand Positive Thinking;* Dan Millman, Jessica Hagy and Chris Brogan.

What life-affirming behaviors do you want to cultivate and strengthen? Hopefully they are the parts of you that are caring first for yourself so you can better connect and care for others. Recall that lesson heard when you're flying: when in danger on the airplane and your oxygen mask drops down, administer it to yourself first so you are able to help your child. In our increasingly technology-connected world, the stakes are higher for acting in mutuality or not. It is harder to hit and run or to push. Instead, we need to pull. Don't break the chain, advises Seth Godin."You can't change what's going on around you until you start changing what's going on within you." ~ Cory Booker

Recognize the Vital Difference Between Kinds of Caring

"There is a big difference between caring about a person (compassion) and putting yourself in the person's shoes (empathy)," writes Paul Boom in *Just Babies: The Origins of Good and Evil*. At our best in cultivating a mutuality mindset, we are not "just" compassionate but empathic with others, not in a misguided "Us and Them" empathy but via "that moral progress that involves expanding our concern from the family and the tribe to humanity as a whole," suggests Bloom.

What aspects of morality are natural to us? Quoting Adam Smith, author of *The Theory of Moral Sentiments*, Bloom suggests that our natural endowments include elements that can be a foundation for strengthening your mutuality muscle:

- A moral sense: capacity to distinguish between kind and cruel actions
- Empathy and compassion: suffering at the pain of those around us and the wish to make this pain go away
- A rudimentary sense of fairness: a tendency to favor equal divisions of resources
- A core sense of justice: a desire to see good actions rewarded and bad actions punished

Yet Bloom ultimately agrees with Thomas Hobbes, who believed that man "in the state of nature" is wicked and self-interested. That's all the more reason for us to constantly exercise our mutuality muscle in every interaction with others and to meditate on that practice just before and after our engagement with others.

The Pain of Loss Has a Powerful, Life-Affirming Purpose for Us

Painful as it is, "our intense agony when we lose a loved one" makes us fully human in our recognition of the ineffable comfort of strong, loving and reliable relationships. How powerfully felt is that recognition of mutuality with another person? Surprisingly, our brains are wired to experience emotional pain, like death of a loved one, or social pain, like being ignored or shunned, the same way we experience physical pain. So discovered the author of *Social: Why Our Brains Are Wired to Connect*, Matthew Lieberman, who followed fMRI studies of the brain. Rather than being a flaw in our brain, he believes that this effect "ensures that staying socially connected will be a lifelong need, like food and warmth." I'm skeptical.

Hint: A mutuality mindset can multiply moments of genuine connection.

Further, that desire is so strong that it refutes the notion of non-conformists, according to Lieberman. Our desire to avoid social loss and loneliness and to connect is so strong that our sense of self is malleable. "Our sensitivity to social rejection is so central to our well-being that our brains" react to social wounds (and ways to heal from them) much as they do to physical ones. In fact, Lieberman alters Abraham Maslow's hierarchy of needs, to indicate that, "social connection is more foundational than biological, physiological and safety needs." That means our need for comforting human connection is more vital to our well-being than even food, water or shelter.

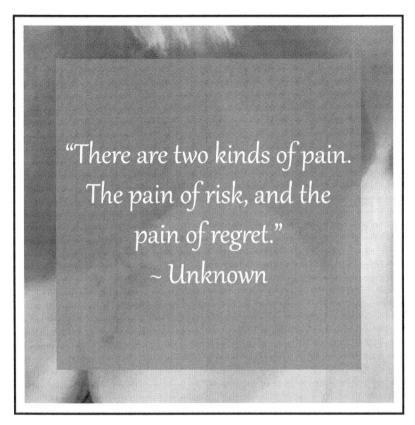

"There are two kinds of pain. The pain of risk, and the pain of regret."
~ Unknown

"The first and foremost instinct of humans is neither sex nor aggression," writes *Love Sense* author, Sue Johnson. "It is to connect. Our need to depend on one precious other—to know that when we 'call,' he or she will be there for us—never dissolves. In fact, it endures from the cradle to the grave. Once we learn that irritability, anger, chronic stress and depression often arise when our attachment needs aren't met, we can begin to heal our relationships, develop more secure bonds, and improve our health."

Recognizing that, the mission of this book is to suggest powerfully simple ways we can connect well with others around our better sides so we bring out the happy and high-performing parts of each other. It is never too late to turn the page to a new chapter and have a more meaningful, accomplished and satisfying life with others.

What Most Matters, Looking Back?

In the longest study of what led men to live happily and successfully to a ripe old age, guess what trait they were most likely to have in common? The lives of 268 men who entered Harvard College in 1937 were tracked for seventy-two years in The Harvard Study of Adult Development. Those who made it into middle and old age as "happy" and "healthy" shared seven traits: mental adaptability to changes in life, advanced education, stable marriage, not smoking, not abusing alcohol, getting some exercise and maintaining a healthy weight. Yet one factor was more important than any of these: Attention to relationships. When the primary investigator on this study for over 40 years, psychiatrist George Vaillant, was asked, "What have you learned?" he quickly answered, "that the only thing that really matters in life is your relationships with other people." It was the social life of these men, he said, "not intellectual brilliance or parental social class" that led to their living successfully to a ripe old age.

In his book *Springboard,* the creator of Wharton's popular " Success Course," G. Richard Shell, offers an approach to finding success that can lead to happiness with others. Beyond cultivating close relationships, to feel happy, Shell cites the ineffable feeling one's doing the right thing, described in two ways. Both are boosted by a mutuality mindset:

1.	*Eudaimonia* is what "Aristotle called the spirit of goodness or the good that we seek for its own sake and not for the purpose of achieving any other good," according to Shell.

2.	Simcha is a Hebrew word with many interpretations, Shell notes, "from simple joy and satisfaction, to the feeling of spiritual exultation" or what Rabbi Akiva Tatz calls "The experience of the soul that comes when you are doing what you should be doing."

3.	Choose Your Role in a World Where Good and Bad Things Spread Faster

In this increasingly complex, connected world, both bad and good actions can hit from more unexpected places and spread farther, sparking more and more varied reactions. Consequently, each of us has the responsibility and opportunity to have a greater effect in this networked world. Thus it is especially valuable to learn how and why we are motivated to do what we do, including our instinct to imitate, our desire to belong and our longing for meaning. Be ever mindful, as Philip Zimbardo's infamous Stanford Prison experiment shows and *Bloodlands* author Timothy Snyder describes, we are capable of great evil.

We are all capable of horrendous and heroic acts, my mission in this book is to offer explicit, actionable ways we can spur each other in living the life-affirming "we" of mutual support in more situations, every day.

We cannot know ahead of time which interactions will deepen into richer relationships, yet we can keep the faith that our mutuality mindset makes every interaction more affirming of each other.

Thus we will experience more satisfying moments that generate more serendipitous ways we are moved to support each other, going forward.

Acting in mutuality makes virtuous circles of collective behavior in our enlightened self-interest – and mutual interest.

We can experience, first hand, that when we bring out the better side in each other, we are more apt to lead a more meaningful and accomplished life *with others*.

It is never too late to turn the page to a new chapter of the adventure story you are truly meant to fully live.

Expect to See More Pandora's Boxes and The Law of Unintended Consequences Becoming the Norm

Illicit author, Moisés Naím was prescient in predicting the rapid rise of self-organized illegal activities – trafficking in humans, drugs, weapons and more. Such nefarious activities are innovating and growing faster than companies or countries, spurring The End of Power, or rather that "power is manifesting itself in new ways and places."

With each innovation, no matter how well-intended, The Law of Unintended Consequences and Pandora's Box effects kicks in. Increasingly such happenings will become the norm, and evil activity can scale, just as good actions can. We can't outrun those twin effects where people may – even with good intentions, invent technology or other systems, ostensibly for just or good purposes, such as drones, that will inevitably be used by others for nefarious purposes.

One horrifyingly example that can affect many of us: Hackers can now hijack mobile phones by getting control of Find My iPhone accounts and holding hostage those account owners who want back the control of their phones, discovered Lisa Suennen. That's the Law of Unintended Consequences of remote tracking, created to find your lost smartphone. Writes Suennen, "Tech hijackers can steal password data, remotely lock iPhones and iPads and then send messages to users saying their iPhones and iPads will be unlocked — after they send $100 to a PayPal account. "

Want to Crouch in Fearful Reaction or Join Forces for Positive Action?

We can freeze in fear, or feel angry and powerless against the seemingly uncontrollable, sometimes destructive consequences of the intertwined twin effects of Pandora's Boxes and The Law of Unintended Consequences.

Or we can see them as another compelling reason to become more adept at motivating others to join forces around specific methods, projects and systems that are mutually beneficial, serving the greater good. In brief, we can adopt a scalable, very human alternative: a mutuality mindset. That means seeing situations through the lens of what, exactly, we can accomplish better together for the greater good. Keep an eye out for methods and systems to adapt to new situations.

You'll want to make a habit of seeking the strongest sweet spot of shared, constructive interest, with the right players to accomplish something greater together than you can do alone. Thankfully that's also a prescription for a more meaningful, adventuresome and satisfying life with others.

We will always face the extremes in behavior – for good and evil – but the temptations and opportunities to act for both will continue to happen faster, more intensely and from more places. It will be a continuing evolution of what carrots and sticks and specific examples we can concoct to reinforce and reward those behaviors that support that mutuality mindset. For starters, recognize that, in our ever more complex yet connected world, luck, randomness and serendipity play a greater role in our individual and organizational success. Consequently, it behooves us to:

1.   Hone our pattern-seeking skills.
2.   Strengthen our capacity to connect and collaborate with people extremely unlike us around strong sweet spots of mutual benefit.
3.   Become more quotable so we can create the vivid context and reasons for others to join in *us-centric co-creation, sharing and collaboration*. Read more about how to capture serendipitous opportunities in Frans Johannson's *The Click Moment*.

Moving from Me to We Is Becoming Ever More Feasible and Vital

Recognize the myth of the lone genius. Instead, capture the humanizing clout of mutuality-centric sharing in all its rapidly evolving forms.

Underlying these many kinds of us-centric structures and systems springing up around the world and swiftly being adapted to other situations, markets and communities is the very human desire to participate in creating something greater together and for each other. You can see those collective actions are happening under overlapping labels: Collaborative Economy, Shareable, Crowd Companies, Social Capital Markets, Crowdsourcing, Mass Customization and more. As a consumer, user, co-creator or other kind of collaborator, you can find several roles to make your life easier and more meaningful with others. At their core, all these actions require a mutuality mindset to succeed. With that approach we are co-creating ways of living and working that can use our best talents together and bring out our better sides, with and for each other.

Get Out of Isolating Feedback Loops and Into Mutuality Circles

More Americans now die of suicide than in car accidents, with middle-aged men leading the deadly pack. One in three Americans over 45 self-identifies as chronically lonely, up from just one in five a decade ago. "With baby boomers reaching retirement age at a rate of 10,000 a day, the number of lonely Americans will surely spike," writes Ross Doughat.

Focusing on finding the "us" in a situation can feel less vulnerable than attempting to attract attention to one's self. That's vital because feeling socially isolated is a slippery slope toward further decline in emotional and physical health. "Lack of social connection is now more deadly than obesity, smoking and high blood pressure," according to a study cited by Emma Seppala. The upside of feeling more compassion, and thus deeply connected to others, includes a stronger immune system, faster disease recovery, less chance of anxiety or depression. In addition, having reliable relationships boosts self-esteem and capacity to empathize, trust and cooperate with others.

"Every time we interact with another person at work, we have a choice to make: do we try to claim as much value as we can, or contribute value without worrying about what we receive in return?" wrote *Give and Take* author Adam M. Grant.

Tip: While strong disagreement exists about whether online relationships boost or hamper genuine relationship building, some technologies, such as those cited at EQ Week, are expressly designed to boost empathic connections, as Joshua Freedman reports.

Satisfy Your Longing for Belonging

As more of us are living and/or working on our own, remotely connected to others at work and less likely to hear human voices as we text and text and email, we crave connection in friendship and in a group where we fit in.

"Go where you're celebrated, not tolerated," is the best advice Marcus Nelson says he ever received. Find where you really belong. As "fitting in" often means shaving off your unique edges, hiding and masking what defines you, discarding any behaviors or appearances or images that prompt others to question you or push away from you.

"Belonging" is about finding that place where you finally let out a deep breath you had no idea you were holding and where you can feel with great certainty that the people around you understand you.

Tip: Find specific ways to acknowledge and celebrate the specific, strongest interests of those you serve and with whom you work or play.

Tip: Joining a group is one of the straightest paths toward cultivating friendship. One unexpected benefit of close friendships is increasing our self-knowledge. That's because they see us more clearly, in certain ways, than we are able to see ourselves, found *Friendfluence* author Carlin Flora. And Julianne Holt-Lunstad's meta-analysis of the connection between social support and health revealed another shocking conclusion: "Not having enough friends or having a weak social circle is the same risk factor as smoking 15 cigarettes a day," so don't make the biggest mistake in friendship: taking them for granted.

Don't Create Barriers to Being in Mutuality

The shocking moment for rising stars is when they meet someone who's rising faster. For some of us this happens in fourth grade; for others it's in college or on a job. The good news is that you still have a way to get ahead. Even now. And it's more fun. Hear how in my conversation with Zane Safrit.

Hint: You may be smart, hardworking, well-intentioned – even good-looking. Yet if you can't collaborate with people extremely unlike you (they don't act right: like you) you're leaving opportunity on the table. In fact, you may be burning bridges.

Four Barriers to Successful Collaboration

1.   *We were raised, especially in the United States, to look out for ourselves first.* The maladapted lone hero who does it his way is a popular figure in our country. Group-centered successes aren't conventional movie plots.

2.   *We weren't taught to create and work in teams.* Luckily, for the past 15 or so years, many students have been studying in groups after school so they're adept at sharing and collaboration.

3.   *Working with others, we lose control.* We are vulnerable to the weakest link, the goof-off or control freak or other wrong team member. Yet, like working alone, collaboration involves a learning curve. You get better at starting simple, sizing up partners, doing more due diligence about them.

4.   Starting conversations by talking about yourself, giving background, taking too long before suggesting the "sweet spot" of mutual benefit when recruiting others.Instead,

describe the opportunity upfront, what's in it for them and what that person brings to the table as a teammate.

Feel Less Threatened and More Empowered

If "just" one caring partner can reduce our reactions to apparent threats, as found by a study titled "Toward a Neuroscience of Attachment," imagine the security and satisfaction of having three friends who expressly feel a mutual bond and belonging to a group with explicitly shared interests and behaviors, where you genuinely fit in.

We can't be experts on our own anymore, because increasingly we don't know what we don't need to know, but others we know do:

- More people are living and working alone.
- Opportunities and problems can be approached faster and from more places.
- What gets rewarded gets repeated. Making an effort to find shared interests with others sometimes spurs them to do the same – with you and others.

Optimize Your Organization's Talents – and Your Own

"If HP only knew what HP knows, we would be three times more productive," renowned former Hewlett-Packard chief executive Lew Platt once ruefully noted. When individuals in an organization have the culture and the technology to easily learn from and support each other, meaning, conviviality and performance zoom up. That's why Deloitte executive Eric Openshaw advocates talent-enabled ecosystems that allow people inside and outside an organization to connect and collaborate in their mutual interest, with apt levels of privacy and tools for finding strongest connects, in real time. That approach enables an organization to optimize its talents. To further leverage that capacity, sustainable companies support their employees in becoming avid, adept ambassadors of the company brand and thus their personal brand. "While we are free to choose our actions, we are not free to choose the consequences of our actions," Stephen R. Covey once observed, yet we can choose actions that boost the chances that others will want to connect, work and play with us.

Perhaps these are sufficient reasons to pull you into the next chapter of your life story, lived more fully and satisfying – with others.

Step Into The Adventure Story You Are Truly Meant To Live – With Us

What was your dominant mood last week? Did you feel exhausted more often than exhilarated? When you're feel stuck, unappreciated, restless, irritated, bored or even angry you are usually indirectly telling yourself it's time to turn the page to a new chapter in your life.

Make your first step fun. See your life as a movie thus far. What genre might it be dubbed? Thriller? Mystery? Romance? Comedy? Tragedy? How would you describe the character roles you most want to play? What are the most frequently-repeated lines and scenes? Do you have a mutually beneficial relationship with at least three of the main characters play the biggest roles in your movie? Are there scenes and characters you'd like to drop? What facets of your character are dormant, yet if more fully realized, would lift up your life to more fun and meaning? What characters would you like to pull in to make adventures more likely to happen? Be primed to step into the mutually beneficial role you'd like to play with others. Here's how.

Become A Greater Co-Author Of Your Life Story

By aptly connecting in mutually beneficial ways, you have the opportunity to use your best talents and resources better to get more done with less effort and more enjoyment. You can stay relevant and sought-after by becoming a Category of One, as Joe Calloway suggests. As you optimize what you know with others, as Marci Alboher outlined in *One Life/Multiple Careers*, thus sometimes *Reinventing You*, as Dorie Clark advocates, you can keep turning the pages of your life story to new adventures In so doing, your mutuality mindset becomes the strengthening and continuing thread that ties your life story together.

As *Good to Great* author Jim Collins discovered, "Being good at something gets in the way of being great." Ready to turn the page to the chapter of the adventure story you are truly meant to live? Want to overcome what Charles Duhigg dubs your "automatic pilot" and flourish?

"Life is like a game of cards. The hand that is dealt you represents determinism. The way you play it is free will." Jawaharlal Nehru

You're most likely to make that move permanent by adopting two powerfully simple practices.:

1.   Picture your specific and compelling reward for succeeding.

2.   Envision other rewards for each step of success along the way.

Nine Steps to Fulfillment

Here are nine steps that have proved fruitful for me, when I actually followed them.

1. Find Your **True North** to Feel More Fulfilled

Make your top goal to deepen mutually beneficial relationships that enable you to use your best talents with others who are too, on activities that reflect your most passionate interests. In this more fully fleshed out role you are truly meant to play, you can experience more meaningful, satisfying experiences with others. You have probably long felt pulled to live that kind of life. Why struggle to fit into an ought-to role for which you are not well cast?

"Our roles in life and problems we face that remain persistently insolvable should always be suspected as questions asked in the wrong way," wrote philosopher Alan

Watts in *The Book: The Taboo Against Knowing Who You Are.*
Seeing your life as a movie and consider what scenes, scripts,
characters and plot lines enable you to flourish. What ones will
you cut from your life or alter? Live your full true self.

2. Recognize Your Own Hot Buttons to See Others More Clearly

As you increase self-awareness, understanding what makes
you run smoothly or not, especially your strongest hot buttons
and desires, you'll finally enable you to

-        Project less onto others, see them more clearly, and
ask for clarification

-        Increase your ability to get glimpses of their
"operating system" so you can discover sweet spots of shared
interest, the path to mutuality.

Tip: The better you know yourself, the better you can see
others more clearly so you can work and play with those
extremely unlike you.

3. Use Your Internal Homing Device?

"It is not the mountain we conquer, but ourselves," wrote
Sir Edmund Hillary. Look inside yourself for your "homing
device" — your most powerful motivation or passionate
interest that can be related to your goal. As Dr. Beverly Potter
wrote in *Finding a Path with a Heart: How to Go from
Burnout to Bliss*, "When we pay attention to our homing
devices and follow their guidance, we invariably feel right
about ourselves and in perfect harmony with people and
activities in which we are involved in the moment."

4. Picture Your Greater Mission and the Adventure It Will Be –With Others

Afraid you'll fail? Supplant your fear with a greater and
more vivid motivation. "A vivid imagination," wrote Aristotle,
"compels the whole body to obey it." Émille Coué wrote, "It is

the imagination and not the will that is the dominating faculty of man. It is a mistake to advise people to train their wills; they should learn to control and direct their imaginations."

Hint: Rather than talking about what you are giving up or how you might fail, reflect upon and discuss the benefits you clearly see.

5. Encircle Yourself With Mutual Support Systems?

To keep your resolve, buddy up with one close friend who's also committed to a new life chapter, and ask up to six others to give you candid feedback and support as you move into the new "movie" role of your life.

The authors of Influencer found that is the only way to permanently change. In *The Healing Brain*, psychologist Robert Ornstein and physician David Sobel found that "the brain's primary purpose is not to think, but to guard the body from illness and despair. Your brain cannot do its job of protecting your body without human contact." Seek out random encounters with people you do not know because they can be "consequential strangers" with whom you can practice the evolving you because they do not know how you usually act.

6. Involve Your Senses To Stay On Your Path

"Thought is behavior in rehearsal," wrote Sigmund Freud. Tie your top goal for your new chapter to your frequent experiences. Write it down. Say it out loud. Associate it with things you see, hear, smell, taste and touch every day. Plant sticky messages on your bathroom mirror, your car dashboard and your smart-device screen. Smell your shampoo and connect it with living that chapter. Brush your teeth and floss and feel the motion toward your new habit. See the result in the shape of your doorknob. As Beverly Sills once told a reporter, "You may be disappointed if you fail, but you are doomed if you don't really try."?

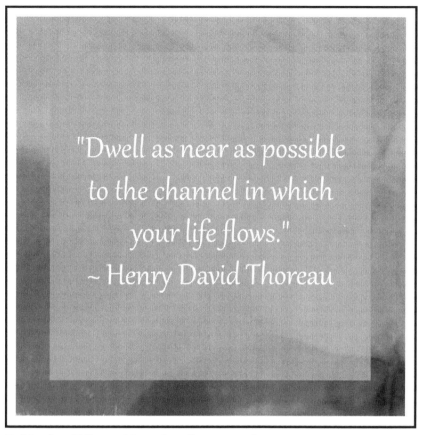

"Dwell as near as possible to the channel in which your life flows."
~ Henry David Thoreau

7. Notice Where You Get Detoured

"The hardest thing to learn in life is which bridge to cross and which to burn," wrote David Russell. Notice your pattern for avoiding your course toward your new life. What activities do you use to get sidetracked? What time of day or day of the week is it most likely to happen? What else numbs you into avoidance? What colleagues and friends help or hinder you on your path? Conversely, when are your stronger moments? Discover these patterns now and you will be more powerfully productive toward this and all the next goals you set for yourself. But don't be too hard on yourself when you're not perfect. As Charles A. Garfield wrote in *Peak Performance*, "On course doesn't mean perfect. It means that even when things don't go perfectly, you are still going in the right direction."

8. Re-Confirm That You're Actually On The Right Path?

As you practice your altered role, parts of you that have atrophied or that you have kept invisible to others may be coming to light. As Jean Shinoda Bolen wrote in *The Tao of Psychology*, "Synchronistic events can assure us when we are on the right life path, and advise us when we are not; at the most profound level, they assure us that we are not mere observers but always participants in an interconnected cosmic web."

9. Plan A Grand Reward?

The bigger the change, the larger the reward you deserve. Enable others who supported you to savor it with you. Get more insights on exactly how from Jeremy Dean's book, *Making Habits, Breaking Habits.* Who knows? Since behavior is contagious to the third degree, you don't know which friends – and friends of your friends' friends – might be moved, by your example, to also turn the page to the next chapter of the adventure story they were meant to live In mutuality with you.

To Stay Grounded, Notice and Emulate Those With Depth Perception

Those who live reflective lives, such as leadership expert Mark Sanborn, tend to notice the nuances in others who are similarly wise. We are prone to having a Third Metric picture of success. Here are two of his actionable observations about such extraordinary people:

- "Their failures don't impact them as negatively and their successes don't get overblown. They let neither success nor failure distort the big picture because they know life is always a mixture of both. They learn from setbacks but don't wallow in them and they appreciate successes but don't rest in them."

• "They make as many mistakes as others but have fewer regrets. Extraordinary people acknowledge they've grown into who they are as much from their mistakes and defeats as their wise choices and victories. To eliminate past mistakes would diminish present wisdom."

"The test of leadership is not to put greatness into humanity, but to elicit it, for the greatness is already there." – James Buchanan

Seek Out Those Most Likely To Have A Mutuality Mindset

Those most likely to be mutuality-minded have traits cited *by Heart, Smarts, Guts, and Luck*, co-author Anthony K. Tjan which I paraphrase here. They are:

• Sufficiently self-confident to be comfortable in expressing their views, yet "their 'talk-to-listen ratio' rarely goes beyond 60 percent. If it does, then "they may be self-important, not interested in learning from others, or conversational ramblers."

• Energy-givers rather than takers who act compassionate, and generous, in short the kind of people with whom you want to spend time.

• Proactive in both solving problems and seizing opportunities rather than resisting, criticizing or ignoring either.

• Not likely to flatter with false praise or try too hard to impress, and thus come across as authentic rather than obsequious.

• Respectful and open with people they do not know or whom may not be valuable to them, what the authors call the "taxi driver or server test."

• Likely to initiate efforts and to persevere as they did when facing financial hardship or other challenge in their formative years.

Self-Aware People Are More Adept at Being Us-Centric, Thus Sought After

Self-aware leaders know their strengths and weaknesses and thus can see others' talents and temperaments more clearly. Consequently, if they so choose, they are more adept at modeling an "us" approach to seizing opportunities and solving problems. They are more likely to optimize their organization's talent and not presume to know what's best for each colleague. They are more likely to realize how powerfully productive and satisfying a mutuality mindset can be for everyone involved.

"It's not about altruism," *Give and Take* author Adam Grant notes. "In the eyes of many people, giving doesn't count unless it's completely selfless. In reality, though, giving isn't sustainable when it's completely selfless. For example, studies reveal that people who give altruistically—with no concern for their own interests—are prone to burnout and depression."

True Humility Attracts Support

The second most significant behavior that differentiated good performers from great performers, based on a five-year study of over fifty thousand 360-degree evaluations conducted on 4,158 individual contributors, was "the ability to work collaboratively and foster teamwork," according to Jack Zenger and Joseph Folkman.

In a global marketplace where problems are increasingly complex, no *one* person will ever have all the answers. That's why Google's SVP of People Operations, Laszlo Bock, says humility is one of the traits he's looking for in new hires: "the humility to step back and embrace the better ideas of others…." "Your end goal," explained Bock, "is what can we do together to problem-solve. I've contributed my piece, and then I step back." And it is not just humility in creating space for others to contribute, says Bock; it's "intellectual humility. Without humility, you are unable to learn."

A Catalyst study backs this up, showing that humility is one of four critical leadership factors for creating a collective sense of belonging. Globally, employees perform better when they see selfless behavior in their managers, such as learning from criticism and admitting mistakes, empowering followers to learn and develop, and acts of courage, such as taking personal risks for the greater good.

Conscientiousness – A Conducive Connector In A Disruptive World

The only major personality trait that consistently leads to success is conscientiousness. People with this trait have fewer strokes, lower blood pressure, and a lower incidence of Alzheimer's disease, plus they commit fewer crimes and stay married longer. Furthermore, they do more thorough work and are most likely to be considered thoughtful by colleagues. Psychologists call it one of the "Big 5" personality traits, along with agreeableness, extroversion, neuroticism and openness to experience. Take a quick Big 5 quizhere.

How do you know if you're conscientious? Conscientious people tend to be more organized, responsible, plan ahead, face challenges well and control their impulses. They demonstrate self-control and "grit," which University of Pennsylvania psychologist Angela Duckworth has found to be more integral to children's scholarly success than IQ. Being conscientious "is like brushing your teeth," Illinois psychologist Brent Roberts says. "It prevents problems from arising."

Tip: Focus on becoming more conscientious, and befriend and marry those who clearly are. One helpful step toward greater conscientiousness is to drop (not temporarily put aside) less important projects or tasks sooner, according to research by *Why Quitters Win* author Nick Tasler.

Get Clear About What's Most Important To You In A Situation

"It is often easier to negotiate with a jerk who knows what they want than a nice person who does not," discovered one of my early mentors, Harvard's Howard Raiffa, co-author of *Smart Choices.* Well-intentioned individuals, even those who believe they are acting in kindness, who choose to not be clear about their top goal in a meeting where decisions must be made, inadvertently make others do more work and feel more stress. Along the way, they cause havoc, confusion and sometimes even unnecessary conflict. Only when you have clarity about your top goal can you be more present and flexible with others.

Opportunity Makers Are Helpful Connectors With And For Others

One habit I admire in many of my friends is cited in a study as boosting well-being in those that do it: We bolster that opportunity for a genuine connection when we introduce people to each other by citing at least one possible sweet spot of shared interest or value.

Identify Your Most Mutually Beneficial Comrades

Attract more opportunities and pleasure by identifying two kinds of friendship circles to strengthen. Identify one circle of extremely diverse people with whom you share a strong sweet spot of mutual interest. In another circle have comrades who can also grow ever closer because you have several strong interests in common. Writing a list of current and potential people for both circles helps you clarify where you might put the most time and attention to grow a more meaningful, accomplished life with others. Use Porter Gale's Funnel Test to discover those with whom you share the strongest mutuality. See where your passions, tone (bold, inspirational, creative) and purpose overlap with others'. Also explore the

5+50+100 rule designed by Judy Robinett, author of *How to be a Power Connector*. I am skeptical of "Dunbar's Number, that we can actually have "150 meaningful relationships" yet believe we can have concentric circles of friends and acquaintances, the so-called "weak links" that often provide value, such as in job hunting or giving other unexpected and generous help.

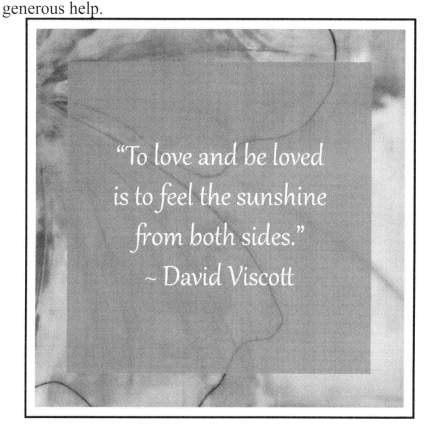

Always Seek To Bring Out Their Better Side

When the Spotlight's On You, Shine it On Others

NBA athlete Kevin Durant, when accepting the NBA award as league MVP, embodied the essence of that recognition. "I had so much help, so many people believe in me when I didn't believe in myself," he said. "We weren't supposed to be here," said Durant, speaking to his mother. "You made us believe. You kept us off the street. You put clothes on our backs. Food on the table. When you didn't eat, you made sure we ate. You went to sleep hungry. You sacrificed for us. You're the real M.V.P." He told each of his teammates, by name, how much their believing in him mattered, writes Ariel Chesler.

Demonstrating mutual mindset traits, Durant was "open, vulnerable, emotionally brave, and sincere" – thus drawing his friends closer and pulling in fans and strangers who felt moved to share what he said and, perhaps emulate the behavior, since behavior (good and bad) is contagious. strangers who heard about what he said and were moved to share what he with others.

Tip: When the spotlight's on you, shine it on those you admire and love, naming them and sharing the vignettes that make that recognition memorable and credible. There's no stronger way to make that spotlight brighter for you, those you name and those who may contagiously emulate your connective behavior.

"The sooner recognition is given, the greater the afterglow" ~ Roy Saunderson

Spontaneously Celebrate Someone You Both Admire

When stopped at a red light one morning, I saw a driver in an adjacent lane crying, as was I. Because we both had our car windows rolled down to capture the breeze on this sultry day, I could tell that he was listening to the same radio show as I was, so I said, "I'm listening too and I feel the same." He smiled, waved and responded, "Some people are nourishing for a long time, eh?" We were both listening to Obama and Peter Sagel's heartfelt goodbyes to Carl Kasell of "Wait, Wait Don't Tell Me." Kasell, a long-time journalism hero to many, including me, was loved for his "bemused gravitas" news coverage on NPR's "Morning Edition."

Hint: Some people, like Kasell, bring out our better side, thus enabling us to feel closer to others when we talk about them. A mutuality mindset fosters such reactions.

Tip: Get close to someone by commemorating a person you both deeply admire.

Take a Hint From Healthy Marriages

People who are happily married for a long time, according to John Gottman, usually have a "magic" 5:1 ratio of positive to negative interactions. Why not attempt to meet or exceed that standard in your interactions with others? Practice praising and otherwise warmly affirming their admirable words and actions more often, letting your instinctively upset reactions slide sometimes. As Keith Ferrazzi would say, show you've got their back.

See Insults as Opportunities to Unify Others Around a Better Alternative

During a Spanish league match, an angry spectator threw a banana at the Brazilian footballer, Barcelona's flying fullback, Dani Alves. Without a pause, Alves picked up the banana, peeled it and ate it. That two-act playlet was captured on hundreds of smartphones in the stadium. It turned a potentially violent crowd situation into a unifying and celebratory scene for those who were outraged by the racist insult. Alves' humorous, unflappable response elevated his stature and enabled him to be more widely known and admired, way beyond the legion of soccer fans. Later the banana-thrower "reportedly" lost his job over the incident, and Alves said he should get it back, giving longer life to his mutuality-centric media story.

Tip: The sweetest revenge is a well-lived life. Turn acts of ill will into healthy opportunities to glue us together around actions of goodwill. One way is to provide a prompt, uplifting, unifying, visible and vivid contrast to someone's negative action.

Before You Say Something, Remember That Negative Feelings Outlast Positive

As Adlai Stevenson said, "When you throw mud, you get dirty." Our primitive "fight or flight" brain still reacts faster, more intensely and longer to negative actions than to positive. Thus even unintentional appearances of criticism lasts longer than praise. If, for example, someone sees five things they like in what you say or do when first meeting you and then, just once, feels criticized, you've probably lost them. That one negative moment may be the most indelible memory and will affect their behavior toward you. That same effect makes most customer surveys worsen customers' feelings about the firm doing the survey. As we answer questions, we deepen our feelings about what we say or write.

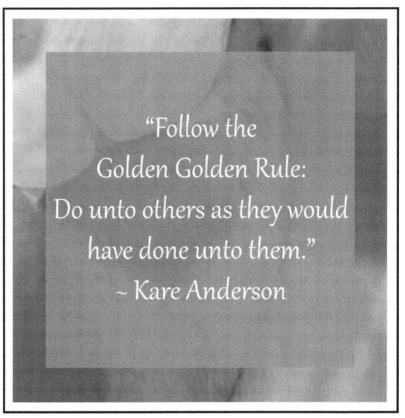

"Follow the
Golden Golden Rule:
Do unto others as they would
have done unto them."
~ Kare Anderson

Design Your Customer Survey to Deepen Positive Feelings

When surveying, in person, in print or virtually, ask the two questions that will reinforce positive feelings of respondents while still enabling you to learn what most matters to them and how you can improve:

"What do you most like about (name the product, service or other topic of survey)?"

"What is one specific example that comes to mind?" (As they get specific in describing that positive attribute and/or experience, they not only believe it more deeply but they also hone their motivation and their capacity to be more credible and vivid in telling others their views.)

Tip: When you start to feel irritated, think of Ian Percy's insight: "We judge others by their behavior. We judge ourselves by our intentions."

Set the Context That Can Foster Conviviality and Connection

In experiments, psychologist David Trafimow and colleagues asked half of the participants to think about how they were different from their friends and family and asked the other half to consider how they were similar to their loved ones. They then asked participants to describe themselves. Those who were asked to think of similarities gave descriptions that included more relationships and roles than those who had thought about their differences.

Tip: To boost bonding, ask people (when they are together) to:

1.   Write down the ways they are like each other. Writing rather than immediately sharing helps slow thinkers keep up with fast thinkers. Fast thinkers aren't smarter, just different in their thinking processes, and each kind has advantages and pitfalls, so they can accomplish more together than to a majority of one kind. **Hint:** Salespeople are often fast thinkers.

2.   Share with each other what they wrote, going around the circle, one by one.

Bonus Benefit: Other studies show that when you reflect on how you are similar to those with whom you are talking, you pay more attention to them. That spurs the other person to listen more closely to you.

"A true leader is not one you look up to because they are the best. A true leader is one that draws the best out in you." ~Anne Warfield

How You Label an Activity Influences How People Act In It

Imagine how the aggressive mindset of participating soldiers was reinforced by the Shock and Awe label for the military doctrine of showing sudden and overwhelming force intended to scare Iraq's leaders.

Similarly participants were swayed in experiments conducted by Stanford psychologist Lee Ross, when asked to play a version of the classic Prisoner's Dilemma economics game. Participants take turns either allotting rewards or extracting penalties according to rules that pit cooperation against self-interest. What they called the game made a big difference in how people played it. Those who heard it was the Wall Street Game cooperated less than those who heard they were playing the Community Game.

Tip: In the first meeting with a team or committee, ask them to each describe one specific reason they are looking forward to working with the others.

Framing the question to pull positive responses from them can jumpstart the Self-Fulfilling Prophecy Effect of being individually motivated to work well with and for each other.

Adopt the Convivial Attitude That You Want Others To Have

"A two-year-old falls down unexpectedly. He isn't hurt but instinctively knows he wasn't supposed to fall," writes Bob Burg, in *Adversaries Into Allies*. "He looks at Mom and Dad for an interpretation of what happened. If they laugh as though it's funny, he'll probably laugh. If they panic and act upset, he will most likely begin to cry. In either case, Mom and Dad unintentionally set the frame that led to the outcome," suggests Burg.

We make that framing choice, consciously or not, many times everyday in our interactions with others. For example, the owners of this business positively framed their request by using unifying humor in the language on their outdoor sign you see to the left.

You can even "re-set" someone's upset reaction toward you, as Burg did when driving in a parking lot and inadvertently almost hitting a man. By quickly waving his hand in friendly apology, Burg shifted the man's mood from anger to acceptance of the "waved" apology.

In every interaction, remember that healthy, happy marriages, according to John Gottman, usually have a "magic" 5:1 ratio of positive to negative interactions. Why not attempt to exceed that standard in all your relationships, beginning this holiday? Practice affirming their positive side and letting negative comments or behaviors slide. Be their soft shoulder.

When in a good mood, we see the positive side of any situation. Unfortunately, the reverse is true too, according to Daniel Goleman. When feeling daunted or down, remind yourself that strengths spread just as fears do. Change the channel in your mind to focus on one of your apt strengths for the situation. Become more grounded and live what Mark Sanborn calls "a reflective life."

For those who do, "Their failures don't impact them as negatively and their successes don't get overblown. They let neither success nor failure distort the big picture, because they know life is always a mixture of both. They learn from setbacks but don't wallow in them and they appreciate successes but don't rest in them," says Sanborn.

"Because I helped to wind the clock, I come to hear it strike." ~ William Butler Yeats

Tip: Suggest that they are acting like jerks, and they will go out of their way to prove it to you some more.

Be Like Them: Brash Friendliness Pushes Us Back, Yet Warm Geniality Pulls Us In

A warm smile tends to beget a smile in return. Yet an effusive, over-the-top laugh and wide grin, for example, may cause an introvert or someone who has just gone through a trying time to back into their shell. So bring out the friendly, expressive part of you that's close to the energy level of the person you are with. Then you are more likely to close the gap of connection rather than widen it.

Make Your Welcoming Expression a Comforting Gift: Avoid The "Screen Face"

As we increasingly look down and focus on what's on our phone, our faces tend to look serious or even dour or dismissive. Unfortunately we often maintain that screen-face expression when we look up to engage with others. Since behaviors create moods and moods are contagious, we are setting up an unfriendly "frame" for the rest of the interaction.

Tip: Adopt the Golden Golden Rule. Do unto others as they would have done unto them.

Be The Gift They Are Happy to Receive

You've noticed by now that some people don't act right, *like you*. That may be the biggest reason we have friction with others. After repeatedly hitting your head against that hard wall, consider finding a doorway through which you can walk to connect with others without that pain. Bob Burg offers this key insight: While it's extremely difficult to change what others believe, you can often avoid conflict or turn around a fractious situation and sometimes even sway others, *if you are willing to "work within their belief system."* He suggests that you view your ego as the horse you ride. If you are in control of your horse, you can "accomplish great things." Conversely, "if the horse is out of control, it can wreak all sorts of havoc, becoming a danger to itself, the rider, and everyone in its path."

Tip: You can't develop positive people on negative feedback.

Enabling Others To Use Best Talents In Doing Good Is Doubling Happiness

For an inspirational example of an all-volunteer, scalable generator of good news, see ServiceSpace's KarmaTube, where individuals use technology to take collective action on specific projects for the greater good. They do so by learning from each other so they can adapt those projects to other situations. This organizational model makes people feel good about participating because they get to use their best talents together on worthy efforts. Such models raise the bar of expectation as we view where we choose to contribute. As Edward R. Murrow once said, "We cannot make good news out of bad practice."

Support Others In Using Best Talents Together On Mutually Meaningful Work

Cornerstone Capital Group's Chief Executive, Erika Karp, told *Purpose Economy* author Aaron Hurst that she "asked her employees whether they had a good day and to identify moments that made it so. She then works with them to refine their job, making small adjustments to change their engagement at work and boost their meaning," an approach that also boosts productivity, esprit de corps and talent retention, according to Teresa Amabile, co-author of *The Progress Principle*, who noted that this effect is most potent when employees feel those moments happen with some frequency. For work and other parts of your life, start noticing when you feel a sense of flow and are pulling in apt allies to co-create something greater than you could on your own. Learn more about exactly how by reading Marcus Buckingham's *Find Your Strongest Life*, written for women yet I believe also helpful for men.

Hint: While we seek meaning at work and in life, we gain even greater satisfaction when experiencing it in the company of others who are doing the same.

Sidestep the Doubled-Edged Sword of Unflattering Comparison

As soon as you notice you are feeling "less than" or "better than" others, step back a moment emotionally. Save yourself from the twin pangs of torment. Instead, Tony Schwartz suggests you follow family therapist Terrence Real's advice: When feeling envious, ask yourself, "How do I hold myself in warm regard, despite my imperfections?" When feeling superior, ask yourself, "How can I hold this person in warm regard, despite his/her imperfections?" or, adds Schwartz, ""What do I truly appreciate in this other person?"

Even and especially when you get intimidated, envious or irritated with someone else, an empowering way to switch moods and perhaps cultivate a connection is to offer apt assistance. "It's actually the difficult situations in your life that make you who you are. NOT the easy ones," believes Adam Rifkin, an inspiring example, in *Give and Take*, of attracting opportunities, influence and friendship, through generous, astute giving.

Tip: What you praise in others is more likely to flourish.

Anchor Your Stories in Redemptive Themes So We Are Moved to Live Up to Them

Are more of your most retold stories anchored by positively or negatively felt incidents? Those who are most resilient, energetic, caring and involved with others tend to link their stories to redemptive themes. The role you most often play in the stories you tell reveals your view of the world, how friendly or hostile, and more.

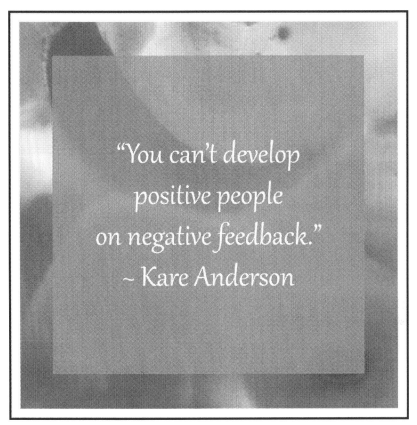

"You can't develop positive people on negative feedback."
~ Kare Anderson

Be a Multiplier Who Brings Out the Smarter Side In Others

Some people may sap your energy and even dull your smarts because they are on the "diminisher" end of the continuum, where "multipliers" are on the other, according to Liz Wiseman and Greg Mckeown, co-authors of *Multipliers: How the Best Leaders Make Everyone Smarter. Diminishers* stifle mutuality. Recognize both by the roles they adopt. Diminishers become Gatekeepers, Tyrants, Know-It-Alls, Decision-Makers and Micromanagers. Multipliers become Talent Finders, Liberators, Challengers, Community Builders and Investors.

Tip: Take a quiz to see if you are a well-intentioned yet inadvertent diminisher.

Help Extreme Narcissists Feel For Others While Growing Your Empathic Instincts

By specifically asking, in advance, someone who's highly narcissistic to feel more caring about the other person in a situation, you can prime that person to feel more empathic when they otherwise would not, according to researcher Erica Hepper. In Hepper's study, extreme narcissists watched "a 10-minute video of a woman — identified as Susan — describing her experience as a victim of domestic violence." In advance they were asked to "Imagine how Susan feels. Try to take her perspective in the video, imagining how she is feeling about what is happening…." After watching, "their empathy suddenly kicked in" – a result that was confirmed via physiological testing to confirm that they weren't attempting to simply look admirable.

Tip: To boost mutually caring, even in non-narcissists, consider making the same request. Whether true or not, act as if you believe that's what they would do anyway, thus supporting their better sides.

Prior to a first meeting of a potential self-organized or assigned team or simply a social setting where people will be meeting for the first time, suggest to individuals you know that you believe they will want to step into the shoes of the people they meet to see the world their way, and you'd like to hear how they feel about what happens in the situation. Asking in advance for that conversation afterwards, moves your suggestion closer to the top of their minds, thus becoming a stronger nudge for their feeling empathic while there. Make this advance nudge a ritual between you and your project partner or spouse, prior to going to meet others. A couple I admire make a point of saying to each other before going out, "Honey, let's step into their shoes to care and share their way, and have a sweet time there."

What's Love Got to Do With It?

Adopt the Michelangelo Effect. That's when couples explicitly and authentically affirm and support each other's best side, thus "sculpting" each other in beneficial ways. In so doing they become deeply committed and enjoy fresh experiences and learning together, according to researchers Arthur Aron and Gary W. Lewandowski, Jr. In psychology, this is called self-expansion – growing through experiences with others into one's positive sense of self.

The behaviors that build sustainable marriages have a mutuality mindset at their core, and could help any kind of relationship become healthier. Those who support each other's strongest talents and introduce each other to new topics may also spur each other and others to self-organize around vital projects where they can use their disparate, best talents together. In so doing, colleagues sculpt each other's strengths as they succeed at projects they could not have accomplished alone.

Such experiences whet the appetite for further deeply engaged work together. Many of the happy couples turned their differences into sources of interest rather than conflict, enabling them to learn from each other. As in a sustainable marriage, three traits are vital: a strongly felt, shared mission; a mutual understanding and expressed support of each other's strengths; and a desire to learn, grow and create with others.

Measure how well you are doing in that regard by adapting two questions from the marriage researchers:

- How much has working with this colleague resulted in your learning and doing new things?
- How much has knowing this colleague made you a better person? Perhaps you would like to take the quiz.
-

Turn An Apparent Attack Into An Opportunity to Connect Better

Notice that your first impulse when you feel attacked is to counter-attack? Or leave? Unless we've had a frontal lobotomy – or a longtime meditative practice – we tend to make things worse. That's because, to survive, our primitive brains are hardwired to respond more quickly, more intensely and longer to seemingly scary, stupid, rude or otherwise negative words or actions.

Consider Hanlon's Razor, "Never attribute to malice that which is adequately explained by stupidity." Replace "stupidity" with a more connective word such as ignorance or miscommunication.

Our hot response usually spurs a spiral up in mutually destructive behavior that's increasingly difficult to cool off. Even if we misunderstood the other person, we are likely to feel justified by their defensive reaction to us.

"If I can't think of at least three different interpretations of what I received, I haven't thought enough about what it might mean." ~ Jerry Weinberg

For the most productive outcome, speak to their positive intent, especially when they appear to have none. You will feel much better if you find out you completely misunderstood the other person, or when you see her cool down in the wake of your warm response to her negative behavior. Even if you sized the situation up accurately and she doesn't cool off, and there are witnesses to the situation, you are showing an unflappable geniality that shines especially bright in the sharp contrast to her difficult behavior.

Hint: You only and always have three choices in any situation: change how you act, accept the situation or leave.

The sooner you make a choice, the less stress you'll experience and less blowback from others for making the choice.

The longer you act the same in a negative situation, the more others harden in their rationalization that they are right and you aren't.

Don't Shoot Yourself In the Foot Over Their Unfair Behavior

All participants in a situation are often more satisfied when they have some freedom to choose the kind of rewards that most matter to them. This proves true at work and elsewhere, as the Ultimatum Game shows.

Let's say, for example that you are handed ten dollars and told you can split it any way you like between you and a colleague. You may value the friendship and/or feel the pressure of observing peers and split the money in half. Both of you will probably feel that's intrinsically fair.

Alternatively, as you and a friend are walking down the street, a stranger approaches and hands you a ten-dollar bill. You may feel okay giving your friend a dollar or two of it. It's found money, given to you, after all.

Here's where we tend to act irrationally, focused on the extrinsic action. About half of those who received money from the one who was given it turned down any offer of a share under 30 percent, even though they knew that meant that the giver could keep all the money and they would get nothing rather than something. And men with high testosterone were more likely to reject a low share when it was offered.

Tip: When making a decision where you could be losing something, pause and consider if you are about to react against the other person or organization's unfair treatment in a way that leads to an unnecessary loss for you.

Benefit From Both Kinds of Motivation

To incorporate the most beneficial mix of intrinsic and extrinsic motivation in decision-making with others, here are two suggestions:

1.   As you learned in the Ultimatum Game, test subjects on the receiving end often reject offers they find too low – even though in so doing they may get nothing. That means you should guard yourself against your instinctive resentment of unfair offers, recognizing that getting something is usually better than getting nothing.

2.   In another kind of Ultimatum Game, subjects who must choose how much to give often offer more than the lowest amount. That means that asking someone to suggest how much he would charge for his product or work means you may have a better chance of getting a deal, as you see it, than if you suggest the price.

"The next time your core beliefs are challenged — try being curious instead of furious." ~ Randy Gage

Make More Friendship, Adventure, Accomplishment and Meaning In Your Life

Who's the Smartest Person in the Room? (Wrong Question)

Bad but familiar advice from an anonymous source: "If you're the smartest person in the room, you're in the wrong room." Similarly, Michael Dell suggests that you "Try never to be the smartest person in the room. And if you are, I suggest you invite smarter people … or find a different room." And well-known blogger, Chris Brogan believes that, "If you do it right everyone around you will be smarter than you." These mindsets actually crush opportunity.

After all, who really wants to be the smartest person in the room if we can find a way to be smarter together than we can on our own? Everyone around you is already smarter than you in some way. Make it a top priority to discover each other's strongest talents – and interests. That opens the candid conversation to using your collective smarts with and for each other.

In any room, let's see if there is sufficient diversity for us to capture the "wisdom of the crowd."

"Star performers cultivate diverse networks, thus tap collective intelligence more than equally smart folks who don't." ~ Alex Pentland, *Social Physics: How Good Ideas Spread*

Make Everyone Around You Smarter For Each Other

Also if you are lucky enough to be in a room with people of distinctly different smarts than you, you can gain more perspectives for solving a problem or seizing an opportunity. That's especially if one of you becomes the "glue" that can hold the disparate group together around a strong sweet spot of mutual interest.

Tip: See and support the best side in others and they are more likely to do the same for you.

Warning: Combat "mirror-tocracy" – or the confirmation bias that blinds us to those who don't dress or talk like us, warned computer design trailblazer Mitch Kapor when speaking to colleagues in Silicon Valley. To hone your capacity to live a mutuality-mindset life, first recognize your top three talents and your top three interests. They probably overlap.

Then understand your temperament across the introvert/extrovert continuum, fast/slow thinking, and optimistic/pessimistic nature. We thrive when in positive contact with others whose way of being is at different points on those continuums.

From that two-part place of self-knowledge you can see others' two parts more clearly and project less onto them, become less reactionary and be more adept at being the glue that holds diverse groups together. That's key to becoming the most sought-after kind of leader in a complex world – the connective kind. You are prepared to see the differences as opportunities to leverage value for each other.

Our Complex World Calls For Connective Behavior

"Diversity trumps ability" as a sufficiently diverse, large group of non-experts often outperforms a small group of experts," found *Future Perfect* author Steven Johnson. In our increasingly complex, disruptive world, we will face more situations where we'll benefit from calling on the so-called wisdom of the crowd. Thus it behooves us to have friends and acquaintances with different life experiences and from diverse professions and industries. Secondarily, hone your capacity to recruit and involve them to support you, as you would support them, and to work together around sweet spots of mutual interest.

Plus, most of us long for meaningful work with others. In fact, more people would rather be part of a productive team that uses their best talents, working on something worthwhile, than to lead, if we had to choose between the two opportunities.

Most sought-after leaders today are, by nature, connective. They become the glue that holds diverse people together around those sweet spots of shared interest, where all the members know why they are involved and what they bring to the table. Looking back on our lives, these experiences will be some of the most memorable.

"Leaders don't create followers; they create more leaders," said Tom Peters. Those who can "flex" behaviors to become the glue that holds diverse teams and new initiatives together will probably become our most valued leaders and partners.

Tip: Become an Opportunity Maker who can recruit the right mix of people in different professions and industries to tackle problems or capture opportunities related to your top interest and talent.

Recognizing Your Many Facets Makes You More Nimble and Constructive

"Complex selves are good for coping with diversity. The more facets you have to yourself, the more tools you have to deal with a variety of circumstances," finds psychologist Patricia Linville. When you appreciate your own complexity, your default assumption about people on the other side of the cultural divide is not that they're incompetent, uncaring or evil. Instead, your first guess is that they are operating according to different cultural cycles.

Tip: When someone does something to which you have a strong negative or positive response, remember they may have a different reason for acting that way than you would have if you did the same thing. Look further to see an underlying pattern so you can glimpse their "operating system."

Move Past Myers-Briggs to Tests That Actually Help You Connect Better

Defining yourself as a certain kind of personality and then viewing others as specific personality types, via tests like Myers-Briggs, can fog your capacity to reduce conflict or work better with others. That's because our "types" usually play too small a role in explaining how we act in the specific situation in which we are engaged. Other factors play a bigger role, such as the nature of the project on which we are working, time constraints, the behaviors the organizational culture supports and so on.

Tip: If you still feel compelled to test for personality type, as millions of organizations and individuals do, according to organizational psychologist and *Blame Game* author, Ben Dattner, then:

Avoid personality or style typologies such as Myers-Briggs, Enneagram, the DISC Assessment, Herrmann Brain Dominance Instrument and Thomas-Kilmann Conflict Mode Instrument that "have been criticized by academic psychologists for their unproven or debatable reliability and validity."

Instead, take tests that better explain variances in your behavior and can also provide you with concrete indications of what to change, such as being set in your ways or easily angered: the Hogan Personality Inventory or the IPIP-NEO Assessment of the "Big Five" Personality dimensions.

Become More Inventive With Unlikely Comrades

Try these two ways to make breakthroughs more often by involving people extremely unlike you:

1. Combine methods or other elements from different domains:

Richard Garfield, the inventor of Magic: The Gathering made $40 million dollars. He combined, for the first time, card games and collectibles (card decks for the game) to create a game that attracted millions of paying players. This is what Frans Johannsen, in *The Medici Effect,* called intersectional thinking. That's combining two unrelated ideas to create something new and valuable.

In the fifteenth century the Medicis, a banking family, attracted to Florence, Italy, (and funded) people from diverse disciplines – including sculptors, scientists, poets, philosophers, financiers, painters and architects – who began collaborating. That kicked off what became known as the Renaissance.

Here's another example: When aerobics instructor Beto Perez forgot to bring his usual music tape to class, he looked in the duffle bag he brought to find a substitute to play. He used his mixed tape of salsa and merengue songs. They not only proved to be popular in class, they also were the unexpected launch of the Zumba dance craze, now the world's largest fitness movement.

Creative people are skilled at "divergent thinking" –"the capacity to come up with many responses to carefully selected question or probes, as contrasted with 'convergent thinking' the ability to come up with the correct answer to problems that have only one answer," found neuroscientist, Nancy Andreasen. She adds, "Creative people are better at recognizing relationships, making associations and connections, and seeing things in an original way—seeing things that others cannot see, that sometimes do not exist."

Just as your top talent has a flip side – your biggest weakness – this insight about the up and downside of being creative can motivate you to closely connect with those with different resources.

Tip: Compare notes with others in different professions or life situations to see how two unrelated products, services, events or other methods could be combined to create something that is more valuable. Also look for ways to adapt something successful in one market, profession or use to another.

2. Encourage everyone to offer specific insights on a project:

Pixar allows employees to participate in the creative process – no matter what their titles are. For example, they screen new films multiple times internally and encourage every employee to give feedback. They also offer after-work programming courses for all employees who want to hone their skills. One janitor took these classes and went on to do a number of jobs at Pixar, including layout work, camera art and voiceovers.

Tip: What if your firm, association or nonprofit set up regular times for cross-functional, candid and facilitated discussions of projects, including potential problems and opportunities?

How Pair-Ups Can Pull Out Our Greatest Strengths

To make smart choices on exactly what to "edit, rather than add," pair up a highly experienced person with a novice on that topic, according to Siam Beilock, performance expert and author of *Choke*. Through working together, one winds up teaching the other and thus gaining clarity on the subject. The other person, writes Beilock, "helps think about the problem differently or 'out of the box' which facilitates the type of creativity that is often needed to solve atypical problems in new, intuitive ways."

Pairing up those with flexible mindsets yet disparate temperaments may also lead to smarter choices. For example, get a rosy-lens optimist to work with a more realistic pessimist, using Marty Seligman's Learned Optimism to confirm who is on the ends of that spectrum. Pair an introvert with an extrovert, using Susan Cain's *Quiet* as a guide to finding both and understanding the benefits that each can bring to the task.

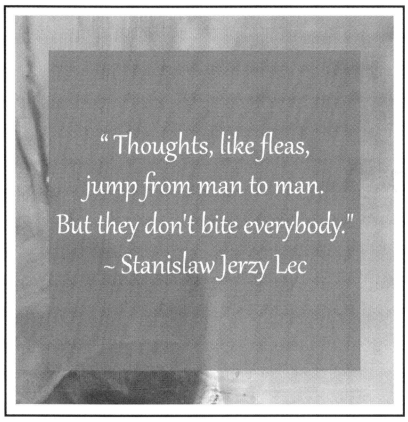

Capture the Clout of Weak Ties

In Morten Hansen's book *Collaboration*, he describes how both weak ties and strong ties are crucial – and that the weak ties created through networking and social media are often the key to new opportunities: "Research shows that it is not the size – the sheer number of contacts maintained by a person – that counts. Rather, it's the diversity of connections – the number of different types of people, units, expertise, technologies and viewpoints – that people can access through their networks." Weak ties help here because they "form bridges to worlds we do not walk within," whereas strong ties are most likely people in worlds we already know. Collaboration,done right, counts at work too, yet is rarely done right. Further, the most valuable relationships are with what Hansen dubs "T-Shaped" people. They freely share across the parts of their organization (the horizontal part of the "T") and deeply within their work unit (the vertical part of the "T").

Also cultivate diverse ties "horizontally" across professions, industries and your various interests, and also hone relationships "vertically" deep in your core area of interest and talent. For example, two of my most valuable relationships when I was a journalist for *The Wall Street Journal* were the CFO – because we had a strong shared interest and extremely different areas of expertise and responsibility – and an analytics expert – because we had different yet mutually beneficial ways of recognizing emerging trends.

Recognize Your Bias to Reduce Your Missteps in Connecting

A story by Harvard social psychologist, Mahzarin Banaji, illustrates this blind-spot bias. A Yale-New Haven Hospital ER doctor was competently stitching up Carla Kaplan's badly cut hand after hearing her tell him she worried that this might hamper her quilting, something she loved to do. Only when one of her students, who volunteered in the hospital, ran up to ask what she was doing in the emergency room, did the doctor freeze. He asked Kaplan if she was a Yale faculty member. When she said "Yes," he stopped operating and "had the hospital track down the best-known hand specialist in New England. They brought in a whole team of doctors. They operated for hours and tried to save practically every last nerve."

Prejudice and behavior often stem from unintentional biases to which we, as good people, are blind. Many of us, for example, are more favorably inclined toward people who are thin, white, young, able-bodied and straight. Worse yet, we are often blind to many of our biases. We create an Us-versus-Them attitude that inadvertently turns our differences into sources of friction instead of opportunities to notice and seize more opportunities to co-create, support each other or otherwise benefit from those differences.

To discover the hidden associations you may have between what you see and what you believe, use the Implicit Association Test (IAT) created by Harvard's Project Implicit. It seems that when forced to make rapid choices on a list, it's "much easier and quicker for us to sort things for which we have a pleasant association (flowers and happy words like 'heaven') than unpleasant (insects and yucky words like 'evil')," according to Anthony Greenwald and Mahzarin R. Banaji, co-authors *of* Blindspot: Hidden Bias of Good People, a book based on this method.

Why does becoming more aware of our hidden biases serve us all? Because "without our awareness or conscious control – bias shapes our likes and dislikes, our judgments about people's character, abilities, and potential," according to the co-authors. Thus we inadvertently strengthen existing systems and behaviors that keep certain groups "in," with more advantages and opportunities, and others "out," with fewer of both.

As the co-authors note, "our friends, neighbors and children's classmates are overwhelmingly likely to share our own racial, religious and socioeconomic backgrounds. When we help someone from one of these in-groups, we don't stop to ask: Whom are we *not* helping?"

Tip: Who are you avoiding, discounting or not even noticing, thus limiting our opportunities to learn, grow and create? We are blindly shutting ourselves off from some people, experiences and opportunities.

The Similarity Bias spurs us, sometimes unconsciously, to keep people very different from us out of our lives. That reduces our opportunities to see the world through more lenses and thus restricts our opportunities and adventures. To benefit from the conviviality and innovation possible in close-knit groups and from diverse experiences, create and nourish small groups within a larger organization and strongly encourage all groups and individuals to regularly meet, mingle and share between groups.

That's what organizations as diverse as Saddleback Church and W.L. Gore have done to boost a sense of belonging, loyalty and capacity to contribute and to innovate with each other. This approach also reduces the chances of groups becoming more extreme, more hardened in their beliefs, and more prone to having an Us-versus-Them, in-group attitude.

That non-mutuality propensity is likely to happen without cross-group fertilization between diverse people and ideas, according to the authors of *The Big Sort*, *Going to Extremes* and *The Filter Bubble*.

Although online filters help us find the information we seek and save us from some information overload, by their nature they also stunt some serendipitous discoveries, believes *The Shallows* author Nicholas Carr. Today's online "birds of a feather flock together, especially online," discovered *Rewire* author Ethan Zuckerman, who says, "This tendency to flock may be keeping us from finding the information we need, and the tools we've built for the Internet only enhance our flocking bias." Online and in-person we sometimes learn more, avoid ruts and enjoy varied adventures and friendships when we look in unexpected places. Living this way also keeps us more flexible, rather than fixed in our mindsets, suggests Carol Dweck, a vital trait when situational changes can hit faster and from more places in our increasingly connected world.

Tip: Be more sought-after by becoming what Zuckerman dubs a "bridge figure" who can "explain one cultural background to someone from another culture." In so doing, you may be the only person capable of keeping a self-organized group together, thus becoming that invaluable individual who can be a sought-after *Category of One.*

Adopt five ways to keep honing your talents, growing, staying flexible and open to new ideas, and pulling in diverse comrades for fresh adventures and opportunities.

Tip: Be the dot connector. Become the MVP-style player in your organization, who supports colleagues in recognizing each other's strengths and becoming sufficiently mutuality- in using them more often. Why? Because, as Glenn Llopis observes, "Sustainable success is a function of how well the employees know each other's strengths and utilize them rightly to maintain momentum.

In the most fluid and high-performing workplace cultures, the differences in people, their cross-functional roles and department duties and the dynamics of hierarchy and rank are perfectly in sync. Simply put, it's about how the 'dots connect' within the workplace's interconnected field of diverse personalities, capabilities and skills sets, competitiveness and expectations.

Since Mutuality of Interests Often Grows Fastest in Illegal Work, We Have a Larger Responsibility to Forge Alliances for Greater Good

As I mentioned in the first chapter, Moisés Naím describes, in *Illicit: How Smugglers Traffickers and Copycats are Hijacking the Global Economy, how* trafficking in humans, drugs and weapons is innovating and scaling faster than any legal industry or profession. More than global corporations or countries, illegal production, trade and money-laundering groups have successfully adopted the much-advocated innovative practices of flattening, self-organizing, adapting and scaling. The situation is worsening at an ever faster rate as the illicit trades become early adopters of those famously touted "social" tools paired with big data – most notably mobile, cloud, crowdsourcing and analytics.

This trend is a major factor in the disruptive decay of traditional power, cited in his newer book, *The End of Power*, illustrating why, increasingly, "no one is in charge" for long – thus making self-organizing skills in forging a mutuality mindset with others all the more valuable and vital.

That leads to two sobering conclusions and a major choice – aka opportunity – for every organization and individual, including you and me:

Conclusion One: Expect the Unexpected And How to Thrive When You Do

Because of two trends in our increasingly complex, connected world, to thrive, you must be able to recruit others swiftly to solve unexpected problems and seize opportunities. You are most likely to be able to do so by being well-known and respected for a mutuality mindset. These are the two trends:

1.   From electronic medical records to drones, increasingly every innovation or action is becoming a Pandora's Box where we must expect the unexpected, for good and/or for bad, and we can't pretend we can control, for long, the unfolding events that will happen.

2.   We are living in a world where good and bad intentions and behaviors can originate in more places, be adopted more quickly, and spread faster and farther, with more varied results. The Law of Unintended Consequences is becoming the rule, not the exception.

Conclusion Two: When Seeking Meaning in a Situation Can Lead You Astray

We seek meaning in most any action, so we sometimes mislead ourselves. Even when shown circles, triangles and other geometric objects randomly moving about on a screen, we tend to give them human attributes. We instinctively determine what their behavior means. Such quick conclusions were sometimes life saving to our ancient ancestors. "It was safer to mistake a twig for a snake than vice versa," suggest psychologists Fritz Heider and Marianne Simmel. Our primitive brain still controls much of our perceptions, yet analytics may alter that instinct.

See Serendipitous Connections That Are Meaningful For You

We can overcome our natural tendency to make the world more knowable and secure by seeking patterns and coincidences where there are none, Kenneth Cukier and Viktor Mayer-Schonberger believe. In their book, *Big Data: A Revolution That Will Transform How We Live, Work and Think*, they describe how our increasing access to the results of big data processing helps us overcome our quick instinct to falsely see correlation and causality, famously described by Daniel Kahneman in *Thinking, Fast and Slow*. As Mayer-Schonberger and Cukier explain, we can "step back from looking at causes and instead look at correlations. Consider the what rather than the why, because that is often good enough."

Then you will have more adventure and opportunity for innovation as well as click moments that lead to both if you cultivate diverse friendships. Citing an example from Ethan Zuckerman's book Rewire,Berkman Center researcher David Weinberger "pointed to the urban planner Jane Jacobs, who championed a style of city design 'to engineer encounters and engagement' in ways that promote diverse communities. I certainly favor structuring serendipity," said Weinberger.

Sensing Synchronicity Can Surface Opportunity

Just as we overestimate our ability to predict how we would respond to extreme stress or how happy we will feel in the future, according to *Stumbling on Happiness* author Daniel Gilbert, it is also true, states *The Click Moment* author Frans Johansson, that "our power of predicting success is essentially zero."

Tip: Get "Pleasure by Proxy." To make wise choices, improve the accuracy in predicting how happy you will be with a decision. Consult someone who has just done what you are thinking of doing, advocates Gilbert, because "the direct experience of another person trumps the conjecturing of our own minds ... because we are far more similar to each other than we realize."

Gilbert dubs this approach "asking a surrogate," which is only "a poor strategy in those rare circumstances where human emotional responses vary widely, such as 'What's your favorite number?'"

In my interview with Johansson, he mused, "It is fascinating how we are so willing to accept randomness in falling in love, the unexpected way it happens, yet we resist believing that unexpected factors affect much of the rest of our lives. Instead, we should welcome the opportunity to understand how to benefit from the serendipitous moments that can spur innovation, and more."

Johansson Gives Three More Reasons to Focus on Finding Click Moments

1.   "The faster the world changes, the faster other people or organizations can catch up with you. The speed of discovering and sharing new business practices, marketing campaigns, products, or services has reached a fever pitch."

2.   "The interconnected universe we are building across cultures, industries, and other barriers makes for a hyper-adaptive environment, one in which a logical approach to

strategy will fare worse and worse when others can easily copy and adopt successful practices, quickly diminishing their advantage.

3.   "But this interconnectedness also increases the frequency of serendipitous encounters and unexpected insight and enables far greater rates of innovation."

Stepping off your familiar path increases your chances of having click moments with disparate people with whom you share a strong sweet spot of shared interest. Reinforcing that notion, *Future Perfect* author Steven Johnson cites research which shows that "diversity trumps ability": in other words, a large, diverse group of non-experts often outperforms a small group of experts."

Like Johansson, Johnson takes an optimistic view of our increasingly connected world. Johnson's complementary prediction is that some of the most positive changes that will unfold in our fast-changing world won't happen because of traditional capitalism or government initiatives. Rather they will come from progressive peer networks, where shared-interest groups innovate faster.

Two of my favorite examples of positive, proliferating innovation and camaraderie that can be experienced within peer communities of shared interest are Quantified Self and Shareable.

Also See Serendipity As A Way to Stay Relevant

Here is another reason to adopt the click-moment approach to your work and life. Meghan M. Biro, in her *Forbes* column, advocates reverse mentoring, a method I believe spurs serendipitous discovery of unexpected shared sweet spots of mutual interest, as well as social learning. Biro cites my former colleague at the Center for the Edge, John Hagel. "Formal schooling and degrees give workers about five years' worth of useable skills," according to Hagel and others at *Harvard Business Review*.

Staying open to serendipitous introductions increases the chances you'll cultivate a flexible mindset, recognizing more sides to a situation and discover more breakthroughs in your areas of strongest interest. Plus you'll open more doors to unexpected happenings in the adventure story you are truly meant to live, with others.

What Makes Click Moments Different From Other Ways of Finding Connections and Ideas?

Recognize click moments in three ways, according to Johansson:

- They tend to occur when two separate concepts, ideas or people meet.

- They are impossible to predict as to when, how or where they will happen.

- You may recognize them because they often evoke emotional responses "such as happiness, awe or excitement."

See If You're a Savvy Serendipity Seeker

If you score above a 36 in the workplace serendipity quiz, you are more likely to be able to lead innovative teams, to "cultivate innovation" and to prosper, according to Earning Serendipity author Glenn Llopis.

Tip: One of the four practices Llopis advocates reflects a mutuality mindset: "Sharing the harvest: Focus on meeting others' needs to improve personal good fortune."

Fertilize Your Combinatorial Creativity by Connecting with Diverse Individuals

If successful scientists "have often been people with wide interests," as Cambridge University professor William Ian Beardmore Beveridge concluded in *The Art of Scientific Investigation*, then you, too, might make more breakthroughs by seeking more varied people and experiences. Innovation most often happens when you adapt an idea from one domain into a new one, and that's most likely to happen when you engage with people from different professions, backgrounds, industries, ages and so on.

As Brain Pickings' Maria Popova suggests, we need combinatorial creativity to have more experiences so we can connect the dots, cross-pollinate. Like LEGO building blocks, "The more of these building blocks we have, and the more diverse their shapes and colors, the more interesting our castles (innovations) will become."

Tips: As *Steal Like An Artist* author Austin Kleon advocates, remix your art with others. Here are some concrete ways:

- Always carry a notebook (or smart device on which you can type or record, whichever works best for you everywhere).
- Dip into other worlds and disciplines by attending a lecture or club meeting or reading publications from worlds quite different from your profession, industry or main interests.
- Create an online filing system in which to put your notes and review it weekly to
- See what fresh ideas are sparked by seeing the notes you recently took.
- Notice the direction(s) in which you are pulling yourself by seeing which folders you use most frequently.
- Consider revising the filing categories in keeping with the connections you are now making between them.

Hint: Bonus benefits beyond becoming more creative and having greater adventures around people unlike you: You improve your memory and motivation for learning more, according to UCL Institute of Cognitive Neuroscience researcher Emrah Düzel.

"Be curious. Read widely. Try new things. What people call intelligence just boils down to curiosity." ~Aaron Swartz

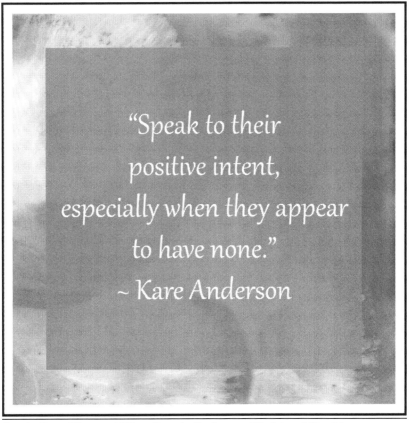

"Speak to their positive intent, especially when they appear to have none."
~ Kare Anderson

Seek Out Those Who Don't Behave Right – Like You

Beginning with our first success in childhood, we become attached to what we believe are our strengths in temperament and talent, which enabled us to win. Why not? They seemed to be what makes us popular. We also are drawn to people who seem to act right – like us. We instinctively project onto them other traits we admire, even when they do not have them. In so doing, we narrow our view on what's the right way to do things, missing many opportunities and friendships.

Are You Neurotic, Open, Extroverted or Agreeable?

Apparently NSA knows. An MIT Media Lab team, led by Patrick Tucker, author of *The Naked Future: What Happens in a World That Anticipates Your Every Move,* found that your metadata – including the way you use your phone, how you make calls, to whom, for how long and so on – can show your personality. To discover and cultivate individuals who are different from you, begin by discovering which of the personality types in the widely used Five-Factor Model of Personality bests describe you:

- Neurotic: A higher than normal tendency to experience unpleasant emotions

- Open: Broadly curious and creative

- Extroverted: Looks toward others for stimulation

- Agreeable: Warm, compassionate and cooperative

- Conscientious: Self-disciplined, organized and eager for success

-

Make Our Differences Work For Us, Not Against Us

As an introverted journalist, I often acted outgoing when interviewing, yet went out of my way to forge a friendship with the chief financial officers in the media outlets that employed me because they acted more introverted. Even so, our multiple differences proved mutually beneficial. Usually CFOs are more linear, measuring success by numbers-based metrics, while my success depended on intuiting what people really meant, what they might be hiding and what to ask whom to get the best and most balanced story, written in ways that even those who were not familiar with the situation could understand and want to read.

Once our CFO and I could find a way to talk so we could understand and trust each other, we found multiple ways we could be mutually supportive. My CFO helped me know what to ask and how to understand reports I received, both when trying to understand a massive anti-trust case and when investigating a complex embezzlement. I helped the CFO set the context for presenting to our company board the need for financial changes in how the company operated. Inevitably, that mutual support fostered learning, a strong friendship and a capacity to be more patient in helping each other.

Why Introverts Can Be Productive Leaders of Proactive Extroverts

"Introverts are routinely passed over for leadership positions," wrote Susan Cain, author of *Quiet*. Introversion is not being shy, reflecting a fear of social judgment, but rather a desire for more time alone, "low-key environments, and fewer yet close friends than extroverts prefer."

Yet, wrote Steve Nguyen, "introverted leaders often deliver better outcomes than extroverts do, because when they are managing proactive employees, they're much more likely to let those employees run with their ideas, whereas an extrovert can, quite unwittingly, get so excited that they're putting their own stamp on things, and other people's ideas might not as easily then bubble up to the surface."

Fast and Slow Thinkers Bring Different Smarts to The Tasks

Whether you are more extroverted or more introverted, you can accomplish more when you collaborate, cross-consult or otherwise connect with those of different temperaments and talents. Another kind of difference is what Daniel Kahneman dubbed fast and slow thinkers. We all do some of both, causing different problems and opportunities in how we make choices, and we can all practice being better at both. Other differences in behavioral styles are described later in the book. Whatever the difference, purposely plan ways people with different temperaments and talents can be heard, appreciated, use their best temperament and talents – and thrive with you.

For example, extroverted and/or fast thinkers tend to bubble up with ideas in meetings, while slow and/or introverted individuals often like time to ponder ideas and write their contributions between meetings.

Pessimistic individuals are more likely to see weaknesses in an idea and be more realistic about constraints in budget or time, while optimistic people are inclined to seem disruptive, suggest big innovations, and get others excited about their ideas. Working together they may often bug each other, yet if they can employ wry or self-deprecating humor about the friction they feel, they can accomplish greater things together than they can on their own.

Every upside often has a downside, however. When something goes wrong for pessimistic people, they are more likely to think it is personal (happened, most of all, to me), pervasive (everything in my life feels wrong) and permanent (it will always be bad). So found *Learned Optimism* author Marty Seligman, who offers practical insights on how to become more realistically optimistic.

The Downside of Up Thinking

As the journalist Oliver Burkeman noted in *The Antidote: Happiness for People Who Can't Stand Positive Thinking,* "Ceaseless optimism about the future only makes for a greater shock when things go wrong; by fighting to maintain only positive beliefs about the future, the positive thinker ends up being *less* prepared, and *more* acutely distressed, when things eventually happen that he can't persuade himself to believe are good." That's why Jeremy Dean believes positive thinking is actually harmful for some people.

Burkeman is onto something. According to a great deal of research, positive fantasies may lessen your chances of succeeding. In one experiment, the social psychologists Gabriele Oettingen and Doris Mayer asked eighty-three German students to rate the extent to which they "experienced positive thoughts, images, or fantasies on the subject of transition into work life, graduating from university, looking for and finding a job." Two years later, they approached the same students and asked about their post-college job experiences. Those who harbored positive fantasies submitted fewer job applications, received fewer job offers, and ultimately earned lower salaries. The same was true in other contexts, too.

Tip: The greater the number of differences between you and another person, the bigger the chances are that you will confound each other and sometimes be in conflict. Before things ever get fractious – and they will – agree that you'll remind each other of your strong sweet spot of shared interest and the value your differences bring to the situation. Perhaps even agree on a hand signal to use when things heat up.

When I partnered, in a start-up, with an introverted analytics pro and a gregarious business development whiz, we agreed to point at our ears and smile, meaning "Let's laugh at what's happening before we scream at each other." It did make us laugh the first time I got upset and they both quickly kept jabbing their ears and grinning. It also dissolved the tension, so we could get back on task. Ironically, four years later I saw them both at a wedding rehearsal where the bride was sniping at the wedding planner. I turned and saw my two comrades pointing at their ears and smiling, adding a much-needed moment of confusion and then laughter to the tense situation.

Discover Still More Ways to Identify Differences Between Us

You need two intertwined habits to be an adept collaborator. First, continually hone your core strength. Second, have a capacity to collaborate with people extremely unlike you.

T-Shaped People Are More Likely to Be Nimble Collaborators

People who have those T-Shaped traits I cited earlier are, according to famous design thinking group IDEO founder Tim Brown, "the backbone of IDEO's collaborative culture. The vertical stroke of the 'T' is a depth of skill that allows them to contribute to the creative process. That can be from any number of different fields: an industrial designer, an architect, a social scientist, a business specialist or a mechanical engineer. The horizontal stroke of the 'T' is the disposition for collaboration across disciplines. It means they have empathy and enthusiasm. Empathy enables them to imagine the problem from another perspective – to stand in somebody else's shoes. Their enthusiasm about other's disciplines motivates them to actually practice them. Thus T-shaped people have both depth and breadth in their skills."

Tip: Use your strongest talents to follow your passion, plus step into others' shoes to see theirs; then suggest seeking a sweet spot around which to work together. With your eye on that shared opportunity, you are both more motivated to work through disagreements or other sources of friction.

Triangle Toward Connecting With Others

Tip: Take the Triangle Talk approach to connecting and reaching agreement with others: You, Me, Us. First refer to their interest, then yours – and then note how your interests coincide. This approach enables diverse people to gain traction sooner toward a common goal. That's the core concept in a book I wrote called *Getting What You Want*, ironically neither the title nor cover I wanted. The book has mutuality-based negotiation tips.

"If you are not willing to follow you are not fit to lead" ~ Vala Afshar

Support Each Other in Making and Breaking Habits

You might make wiser decisions, glean fresh insights about how to change a habit, and recognize better ways to connect with those who have different approaches to expectations by using Gretchen Rubin's character index. It will be at the center of *Before and After*, her book about good and bad habits. She self-describes as an Upholder married to a Questioner.

- **Upholders** respond readily to outer and inner expectations (I'm an Upholder, 100%).

- **Questioners** question all expectations; they'll meet an expectation *if* they think it makes sense.

- **Rebels** resist all expectations, outer and inner alike.

- **Obligers** meet outer expectations but struggle to meet expectations they impose on themselves.

Work Well With Three Archetypes Typical in Different Parts of the United States

In their research of different regions of the United States, teasing out psychological characteristics of extraversion, agreeableness, conscientiousness, neuroticism and openness, University of Cambridge psychologist Jason Rentfrow and his colleagues came up with the following three profiles, admitting to limits in their conclusions. Still, recognizing which profile most fits you can enable you to cultivate people who seem to fit the other categories to get you more insights on situations that most matter to you:

Friendly & Conventional: "In many respects, the Friendly & Conventional region reflects Middle America, or 'Red' states," write the researchers, and the F&C region, which includes basically the entire Midwest, "comprises predominantly White residents with comparatively low levels of education, wealth, economic innovation, and social tolerance." These folks tend to be "politically conservative, religious, and civically engaged."

Relaxed & Creative: "The Relaxed & Creative region comprises predominantly states along the West Coast, Rocky Mountains, and Sunbelt." An educated, disproportionately non-Caucasian part of the country, R&C's "psychological profile is marked by low Extraversion and Agreeableness, very low Neuroticism, and very high Openness." It's a region "where open-mindedness, tolerance, individualism, and happiness are valued" – so it's perhaps unsurprising that it's experiencing positive net migration.

Temperamental & Uninhibited: This is the mid-Atlantic and the Northeast – "quintessentially Blue states." The region is characterized by "low Extraversion, very low Agreeableness and Conscientiousness, very high Neuroticism, and moderately high Openness…. There are disproportionate numbers of older adults and women in this region, in addition to affluent and college-educated individuals."

Are You Limiting Options as a Specific Versus Holistic Perceiver?

As Bae Pak from Korean motor company Kia told Erin Meyer, "When we work with Western colleagues, we are often taken aback by their tendency to make decisions without considering the impact on other business units, clients, and suppliers."

When asked to view 20-second animated videos of underwater scenes in a study, Japanese and American study participants focused on different things. Americans most frequently cited the bright-colored, fast-moving fish and other things in the foreground, while Japanese described the interrelationships they saw between the fish and other objects throughout the video.

When asked to take photos of someone, the Japanese were more likely to include the surrounding environment in the photo, while Americans were inclined to take close-ups of the face. In these and other experiments Asians tended to look at the holistic context, go from macro to micro in viewing a situation. Conversely, Americans were more likely to look at what they thought were the main parts of the scene first and interview participants individually rather than asking the team to spend time coalescing around a goal or problem to build unity within the team. This is a kind of fundamental attribution bias.

Tip: Avoid attention blindness. When you or others are describing a problem or opportunity, notice if you are including the larger context in which the situation and players exist.

Are stepping far enough back to see all the factors that need to be considered when deciding how to tackle the problem or seize the opportunity, and then consider what kinds of expertise and contacts you need to accomplish your goal. And, of course, involve diverse and holistic thinkers, to be sure you are doing both.

Be The Glue That Bonds Us Together

Here's a startling and discomforting way I learned about the hidden power-attracting clout of mutuality. For recruiting, interviews are notoriously inept ways for us to identify apt employees, allies or teammates.

We tend to like people like us, those we interview early in the day, or those who are attractive or can easily look genuine. Instead, why not see how they perform with others? That's what I learned when asked to play the Triangles Game

How You Explore Determines What You Discover

I played the Triangles Game as the last step the Coro Foundation used to select Fellows for its public affairs program.

All final applicants were seated in groups of six around round tables. In front of each of us was placed a varied set of triangle-shaped cards. The board chair stood up in front of us all and said, "There is only one goal to this game and only three rules. The goal is to see which team finishes first. To finish, each of you at your table will have assembled in front of you a set of the triangles that fits to create a larger triangle. The first rule is that you can give a piece to get a piece to fit into your mix; yet you cannot ask for the piece you want back in trade.

Two, you have to accept any piece that is offered to you. Three, you cannot talk until the game is over because a team has won."

What ensued was unforgettable, especially in retrospect after we heard the Coro leaders describe the kinds of behaviors we, like many before us, displayed when playing this game. For example, some individuals, in their ardor to win, couldn't help but point to the card they wanted. Some, as they came closer to completing their overall triangle of cards, muttered requests and pointed. After just a few trades, almost all of us instinctively kept looking down at our partially assembled set of cards and looking for what was missing and who had one of them.

Our team won, and certainly not because of me but because of Sue Wong (yes, that is her name), who sat next to me. Unlike the rest of us, she was looking at what cards were missing in front of each of her teammates' mix of cards. Then she was looking down to see which card she had that might help one of us complete our overall triangle of cards, and accepting the discards from us. Eventually she was orchestrating the completion of each teammate's triangle by aptly sharing the discarded cards she received to the right member. In so doing she facilitated our winning. She played the mutuality-mindset "card" of behavior better than anyone else on our team or the other teams. Everyone received an indelible first-hand experience of the power of mutuality behavior after the wise Coro leader drolly described to all of us in the room what we had done "together."

Tip: "Don't be a sheep, be a shepherd." ~ Yael Citro

Cite a Strong Talent in Each Teammate Even if You Aren't the Leader

When I was a *Wall Street Journal* reporter, my bureau chief bluntly told me one day that I took too long when interviewing some people, and sometimes that was a good thing. I got insights about the interviewees' views on other topics. He told me that, when I finished writing the story I was assigned, I should write notes on those other opinions I heard. Then in future stories, I might see where one of those interviewees had an unexpected yet relevant angle and quote them. In effect, he showed me a talent I did not know I had, that I saw patterns between apparently unrelated things people said. That insight was life changing for me. (He was also extremely direct in describing my shortcomings and ultimately became a sponsor.)

Consequently I developed a habit of telling others when I saw them demonstrate a talent that appeared to be hidden to them.

Vividly and specifically praise others when they shine a spotlight on individuals who are showing their strengths. In so doing, connective leaders can contagiously create close bonds and model connective behavior that embodies the sentiment Rosabeth Moss Kanter advocates for leading: "I stand behind you. My job is to make yours successful."

When They Make a Mistake, Enable Them to Save Face and Self-Correct

What if Jennifer successfully completed a project that was vital to the division you supervise, yet left colleagues in the lurch on other projects – without telling them? You have an opportunity to offer a vital team-values lesson. Act as if she understood she'd made a mistake. Meet with her privately and say, "I appreciate your great work on that project. And I know you feel badly that your colleagues didn't learn, in time, that they would need to rapidly make adjustments to get the other projects completed. In our next meeting, how do you want to explain to them how you will do things differently in similar situations in the future? You have strong talents and I want to fully back you in gaining their support."

Tip: As a mutuality minded leader, demonstrate that being a strong team player is as important as being a rising star and act as if that is also their intention.

That way you can sidestep the need to criticize to correct their mistakes while making it crystal clear that they *get to* acknowledge their mistake to their peers who were most affected and say how it will not happen again.

Collaborating With Diverse Individuals Is Not Easy – Just Vital

After seeing the anonymously sent photos of frightened women packed in the bottom part of the freighter, destined for sex slavery, an ex-diplomat hastily assembled our team. We were intensely dedicated to finding out who was profiting from the human trafficking – and to expose them. Three countries wanted to find out, and so did my newspaper. Ironically, conflict soon cropped up within our team as we followed the money trail and almost sabotaged our work.

Yet the ways we ultimately got in sync and succeeded may hold lessons for any diverse team. Our group also included a former computer hacker, an ex-counterintelligence officer and an international banker.

The problem was that no one acted right – like me. And we all felt that way. It wasn't just our talents but also our different temperaments that were in the way. Among us we had introverts and extroverts, fast and slow thinkers, and pessimistic and optimistic mindsets. And we'd been recruited to this project, so we began as strangers to each other. Yes, we did find and expose the illicit network. Although that was several years ago, it remains a vivid memory to this day. Thriving in diverse teams is key to accomplishment and meaningful work in our increasingly complex yet connected world. "The collective capacity to make good calls and wise moves when the need for them exceeds the scope of any single leader's direct control," suggests Tom Davenport in *Judgment Calls*.

Make Your Differences Work For Everyone in the Group

Why not be a connective leader, the invaluable glue that holds such groups together? Here are some methods that helped us:

1. Experience the Freedom of Agreed Upon Constraints
To create a common ground on which we could get more done with less friction, we agreed on a few simple rules, including that we could agree to change rules as we went along. Since a newly-formed team is not accustomed to working together, it has not yet developed bad or good team habits. To get off to a positive start that can endure, it helps to

have some mutually agreed upon boundaries. It grounds a team and thus leverages shared comfort during those boundless times of co-creating. These were some of our rules:

- Always have a prioritized agenda when meeting. That doesn't mean that, once at the meeting, you can't agree to collectively alter it. Yet starting with something concrete is easier to alter than starting with nothing.

- First, say why you are bringing a topic up and what you want from the group before diving into it.

- Do not negatively personalize the discussion. For example, don't say "That is stupid."

- Always directly respond to a question rather than giving background first or changing the topic.

- Whenever possible, do not just disagree; offer another option.

2. Meet And Decide in Conversation And In Writing

Slow and fast thinkers can be equally smart. Fast thinkers flourish in conversation, and slow thinkers benefit from time for deliberate thinking and then writing, as Daniel Kahneman famously describes in *Thinking, Fast and Slow.* A smart team provides for both needs. Further, introverts thrive with adequate alone time and deep relationships with a few friends, as *Quiet* author Susan Cain explains. Extroverts prefer to be engaged with people more often and enjoy having a wider circle of friends. Introverts also need down time to think and gain faster support from their close friends. Extroverts still get the face to face time they want to get things done and be better able to tap the wisdom of crowds for insights, because they have a wider group of contacts.

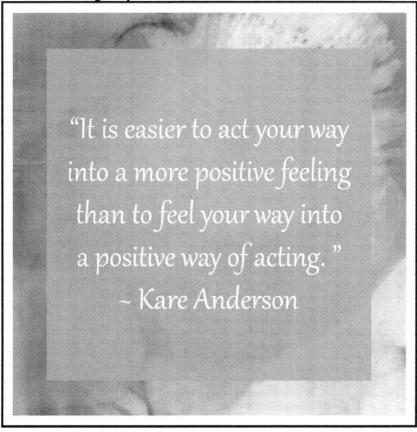

"It is easier to act your way into a more positive feeling than to feel your way into a positive way of acting."
~ Kare Anderson

3. Consider Both Best And Worst-Case Scenarios

Optimists often tend to view situations through a rosy lens, minimizing or ignoring possible obstacles, yet tending to be more tenacious in overcoming them. When a problem arises, pessimists are more likely to see it as permanent (it will always be this bad), pervasive (everything, not just this problem, is bad) and personal (it affects me the most). While they are inveterate doubters, they are also – according to some research –more realistic in their view of a situation than are optimists. Thus, discussing both extremes of what might happen when choosing a course of action can lead to smarter, collective decision-making.

4. Praise Specific Actions of Teammates, Especially Those Extremely Unlike You

Just like smiling (or even slightly elevating your eyebrows) not only raises your mood and likeability – and that of those facing you – authentically praising those who think and act differently than you makes you feel both more likeable and more familiar to each other. Thus you are more likely to focus on the convivial, helpful parts of your work together rather than on the fractious moments – making more productive times a self-fulfilling prophecy. This approach also reduces the natural instinct to for each of us to believe we are doing more than most others, according to *Mindwise* author, Nicholas Epley.

Keep Reminding Yourself of the Power of Unlikely Allies

Even if you experience success with unlikely allies, it's all too easy to slip back into hanging out just with those who act and think much like you. To reinforce your motivation to cultivate diverse colleagues and be adept at recruiting and leading teams of diverse people, be prepared with the bad and good news. "People in diverse groups are less happy. Their views are challenged, and they feel like the outcomes were manipulated. Based on their experiences, they will self-report that it was not better than when they were on a homogenous team," *The Difference* author Scott E. Page told angel investor Steve Jurvetson and others at a Santa Fee Institute meeting.

Yet when diverse teams experience success they know wouldn't have happened without each other, they tend to form strong bonds, so it's well worth finding out how. The key to being smarter together than as individuals is that the group is sufficiently diverse that they "got stuck less often than the smart individuals, who tended to think similarly," according to Page. Reinforcing that research, a recent Deloitte study cited by Alison Griswold found that "diversity of thought" spurs "innovation and creative problem solving" and reduces "groupthink."

Participate in tight-knit teams that regularly interact with other teams. In so doing, you gain the benefits of staying nimble, engaging with people you get to know well, while avoiding becoming extreme and hardened in your beliefs and methods as happens when teams act in continued isolation from others.

Record What's Most Significant in Each Experience With Others

"Immediately after every lecture, meeting or any significant experience, take 30 seconds – no more or less – to write down the most important points you heard" is advice Robyn Scott passes along from an anonymous "éminence grise of the business world." Don't consider this note-taking but rather "an act of interpretation, prioritization and decision-making," she suggests. Fostering your mutuality mindset, this habit helps you crystallize core ideas. You are more likely to actively listen, ask better questions and offer relevant help in the current conversation. As well, you are better able to recall and refer to apt insights and more ready to adapt them to other situations.

Tip: What specific virtues – no more than seven – would you suggest to others at your workplace, family, club, organization family or circle of friends to adopt as mutually accountable, meaningful traits to guide "our" behavior?

Ten Ways Mutuality-Mnded People Strengthen Self-Organized Teams

Creating self-organized teams will increasingly become the norm, not the exception, in nimble, sustainable companies, clubs and other organizations. Synthesizer-style leaders are best prepared to jump start and facilitate such teams. By emulating their traits, you can become sought-after. Plus you'll inevitably tap more opportunities to learn and cultivate meaningful friendships in work and other parts of your life.

1. Choose the Right Team Members for the Task

Then tell the team why each member was chosen, the specific talent and experience that person can provide. After they have met together, ask if they believe they are missing any kind of team member to do the task.

2. Be Very Specific in Describing the Team's Top Goal

Then ask the team if there is a better goal in light of the organization's top goal. Be sufficiently specific that success or lack of it is clear. For example, a goal may be to attract referrals from five percent of our customers within a year.

3. Characterize the Individual and Collective Benefit of Participating

Vividly and concretely characterize the direct benefit to the listeners up front, for providing support, even if it is a part of their jobs anyway. Then characterize how the expected support directly relates to a top goal of your organization.

4. Give the Team the Power and Responsibility to Self-Organize for Their Success

Tell the team to propose how to accomplish that goal and how they want to be held accountable, to each other and to you. Within a week after the team is formed, ask them to report their approach. Listen deeply, questioning to be sure you understand, yet rarely to suggest an alternative. Teams will work harder and smarter to prove *themselves* right than to prove you were, and they will become proud of each other and the opportunity you entrusted in them. As well, ask what rules of engagement they will use to work together, what resources they need, their timetable and preferred way to keep you in the loop as they proceed.

5. Go Slow to Go Fast?

At the beginning of every meeting or other interaction, do everything lower, slower, less – in moving and speaking – so you get "in sync." You can then establish a common direction and involvement so when you pick up speed later on, everybody is eager to be on board.

6. Play It Straight?

Announce some clear, actionable rules upfront and rewards for participation. Don't change them midstream without a compelling reason that those affected can believe.

7. Play it Back?

Seek and reward candid feedback on an ongoing basis, and respond specifically and soon to what you've been told, including the rationale about the action you will or will not take, based on that feedback. ??

8. Synthesize the Best?

Listen. Ask. Ask more. Then synthesize others' ideas as a way of proposing the next course of action, citing others for their specific insights that enabled you to forge this approach.

9. Give Third-Party Endorsements?

Give specific, genuine praise for others' contributions, from anywhere in the company. Praise them virtually and in front of those who are important to them, and in ways that reflect their highest self-image and values – and their strongest talents and temperament.

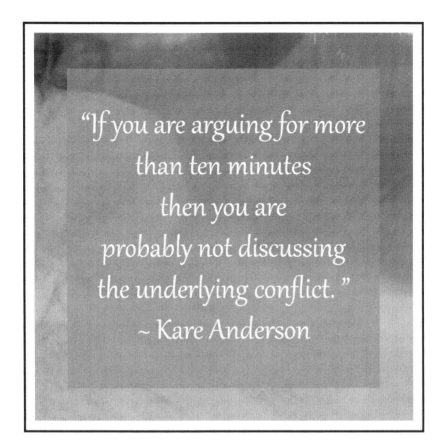

"If you are arguing for more than ten minutes then you are probably not discussing the underlying conflict."
~ Kare Anderson

10. Walk Your Talk?

Demonstrate congruency in all you do. Make and keep agreements. Reflect a clear set of actionable, core values that you keep, regardless of whether they share those values.

"In everybody's life, at some time, our inner fire goes out. It is then burst into flame by an encounter with another human being. We should all be thankful for those people who rekindle the inner fire."~ Albert Schweitzer

Boost Understanding, Competence and Connection: Keep Messages, Rules and Requests Simple And Brief

Story: "Why do emergency room doctors tend to over-diagnose heart attacks in older and overweight people, and under-diagnose them in women and younger people?" asks *The Leap* author, Rick Smith. Because the weight, age or sex of the patient spurs doctors to consider "all sorts of tangential assumptions that cloud the reality before the doctor's eyes." Instead, he advises them to first look for no more than the four most common signs of heart attacks and then consider more variables. Research shows that ER doctors are dramatically better in making a successful diagnosis when they do.

Similarly, "the simpler business metrics are, the easier they are to grasp and translate into useful activity," according to former Bain & Company director and author of *The Ultimate Question*, Fred Reichheld. For example, rather than using "long, involved surveys" to measure customer satisfaction, Reichheld suggests "reducing the metric to a single 'ultimate question,' rated on a one-to-ten scale: 'Would you recommend us to a friend?'"

Lesson: This may sound prosaic at first, yet simplicity and brevity can only be accomplished via clarity, willingness to prioritize (including letting go of some goals) and stepping into the shoes of the people you seek to lead, sell to or otherwise sway. As a connective leader, distill your core mission of your firm or team to an actionable, relevant goal so others are more likely to understand and remember it, and use it as a useful guide for your decision-making. Few people who seek to lead manage to do this.

Become a Stronger Pattern Seeker and Meaning Maker
Story: From supporting the creation of "solar libraries" so impoverished students in the Philippines have access to light to launch experiential design-thinking classes for at-risk youth in the Bay Area, projects are receiving LinkedIn funding because the company asks its employees to be "our eyes on the ground; as current volunteers and Board Members," writes Ariana Younai. And that's just one of the programs she described as part of their LinkedIn for Good for Employees innovation and transformation grants. See how LinkedIn is visibly leveraging its employees' strongest talents and interests as a way to make a meaningful difference in the world and for the firm.

Tip: Identify a "noble shared purpose" with those you lead, or seek to lead, and then advocate a way to "co-create value with them for the larger society," suggests *From Smart to Wise* co-authors Prasad Kaipa and Navi Radjou. In so doing you are more likely to evoke their happier and higher-performing behavior together as they "keep their eyes open for what connects and integrates each other and their larger purpose," the co-authors discovered. "Organizations driven by purpose and values outperformed the market fifteen-to-one and outperformed comparison companies six-to-one, according to *Build to Last* co-authors Jim Collins and Jerry Porras.

As a connective leader in this way, you also evoke added benefits via what I dub "The Halo Reinforcement Effects." As Hoffman vividly summarizes the pro bono work and funding of his firm, he not only burnishes the company brand and extends its positive visibility in ways that boost enduring customer loyalty in the way *The Human Brand* authors cite, but he also reinforces the continuance of admirable behavior in proud LinkedIn employees. Plus, as the team at *Huffington Post* has discovered, we are especially prone to share good news. Three more lessons we can learn from connective leaders: Notice how they step in the shoes of those they seek to lead, exude warmth first and then competence, and are deeply connected and widely quoted.

Take the Bright Way to Make a Bad or Good Situation Better

When told to tackle the widespread child malnutrition in Vietnam in 1990 as an employee of Save the Children, Jerry Sternin could easily have become overwhelmed. Plus the country's foreign minister told him, "You have six months to make a difference." Instead of looking at the macro problems such as polluted water, he asked the mothers in one village to meet with him, to discover, together, the healthiest children and to then discover why.

They found that mothers of healthier kids were feeding them four meals a day (using the same amount of food as other moms but spreading it across four servings rather than two). The larger twice-a-day meals eaten by most families turned out to be a mistake for children because their malnourished stomachs couldn't process that much food at one time," according to Switch co-authors Dan and Chip Heath. They characterized this approach as searching for "a bright spot and then cloning it." Rather than trying to fix what's wrong, it's easier to scale what's going right.

Tip: Look for the positive deviance in a situation and see how to spread it.

To remember this, picture someone riding an elephant, Chip Heath suggests, citing psychologist Jonathan Haidt's metaphor. "The Rider represents our analytical, planning side. The Rider decides, 'I need to go somewhere, here's the direction I want to go,' and sets off. But it's the Elephant, the emotional side, that's providing the power. The Rider can try to lead the Elephant, but in any direct contest of wills the Elephant is going to win – it has a six-ton advantage."

Tip:

1.   Look closely at the situation you want to fix or improve and ask these key questions:

•   What's working well now, and how can we do more of it?

•   In the midst of this mess, who is thriving and how can we help others thrive like them?

2.   Once you discover one or more sweet spots, consider what other talents and resources you need to make such shining situations the rule rather than the exception. The Heaths call this copying success rather than solving problems. Seeing something you want to fix, instead of troubleshooting, this is success-spreading.

Finding the things you're doing right, as an individual or a team, and figuring out how to do them more often is considerably more pleasant and likely to succeed than feeling guilty for what you're doing badly and attempting to stop it.

See Soft Ways To Make Strong Connections

Cultivate the Self-Deprecating Humor That Creates Conviviality

Coming into a tense team meeting, Jake Torkelsen announced, "I had an IQ test. The results came back negative." Self-deprecating humor can pull others closer, even in unexpected kinds of work. Whether you are seeking support, selling your product, forging a partnership or even considering marriage, it can be a key tool to knowing if and how to proceed. The *right kind of humor* is the best lubricant to smooth your way in life, pulling in opportunities and friendship.

Before Offering to Collaborate, Discover How Open They Are to Others' Ideas

After watching Cesar Milan the famous "dog whisperer" Paula Poundstone learned that "when a dog is sniffing you, he's gathering information." She concluded that "My dog is collecting an extensive dossier on me." How we evoke and respond to humor is one of the strongest indicators of how flexible, open and fun we will be with others. Using humor, you can see how they view themselves and their world. That's helpful information if you are thinking of collaborating with someone – or even considering whether to get to know them better. "A well-developed sense of humor is the pole that adds balance to your step as you walk the tightrope of life," wrote William Arthur Ward.

> "If you give enough other people
> what they need in their lives
> you often get what you need,
> sometimes even before
> you know you need it
> and sometimes from individuals
> you did not know
> could provide it."
> ~ Kare Anderson

Kid About A Common Situation

"The next best thing to solving a problem is finding some humor in it," mused Frank Clark. "Executives with a sense of humor climb the corporate ladder more quickly and earn more money than their counterparts," according to *The Harvard Business Review*. Women say they want someone who makes them laugh. Men want someone they can make laugh.

Tip: Hearing what's funny in a group also enables you to understand what isn't safe to laugh at.

Avoid Humorless People

"The ultimate test of whether you possess a sense of humor is your reaction when someone tells you that you don't," advises Frank Tyger. How do we get that way? "By starving emotions we become humorless, rigid and stereotyped; by repressing them we become literal, reformatory and holier-than-thou; encouraged, they perfume life; discouraged; they poison it,'" warns neurologist Joseph Collins.

Without humor it is hard to step back to see a situation in a brighter way or come to terms with it – or to hope. "There is a sorrow in the seriousness of humorous people. They do not easily find among ideas or purposes a place of rest. The courage in their eyes is wistful.

Tip: Those who don't recognize irony or self-inflicted sarcasm, may lack higher cognitive skills.

Evoke Unifying Humor

After the mad cow scare, a man in Montana made this bumper sticker: "Montana – At least our cows are sane." What slant on the situation can you offer that makes us laugh in recognition of a shared value, exploit, or even a droll acknowledgement of where we messed up together or of a partner's foible? Numbers are not my strong suit. After I used a hand calculator to add up the figures for a project budget and came up with three different totals, my business partner quipped, "There are three kinds of people: those who can count and those who can't."

Tip: When your humor highlights positive traits or past experiences we have in common, you and I grow closer. Kidding *with* co-workers builds bonds.

When You're the Honcho, Hero or Current Center of Attention, Help Them Feel Co-Equal

Self-deprecating humor is disarming and makes others feel more included, as hockey player Chris Pronger managed to do when talking *with* reporters. That's especially helpful when others may have reason to feel in awe of you or ignored by others in the situation.

Tip: Reach out to the person who is most ignored in the meeting, social mixer or other gathering, especially when you are the center of attention, and you may make an ally for life.

Avoid or Upstage Cutting Humor

Groucho Marx drily groused, "People say I don't take criticism very well, but I say what the hell do they know?" Most of us rationalize our use of cutting humor as harmless fun. It is usually a matter of perspective. Who is being skewered. As Mel Brooks concluded, "Tragedy is when I cut my finger. Comedy is when you fall into an open sewer and die." Unifying humor is healing and enables us to see the larger picture of something better for us all.

See more ways to cultivate mutuality via humor by reading "Are Funny People More Successful In Business?" by Jenna Goudreau; "8 Tips for Using Workplace Humor" by Mike Myatt; and "Five (Serious) Tips for Using Humor to Connect, Engage and Influence" by Mark Ivey.

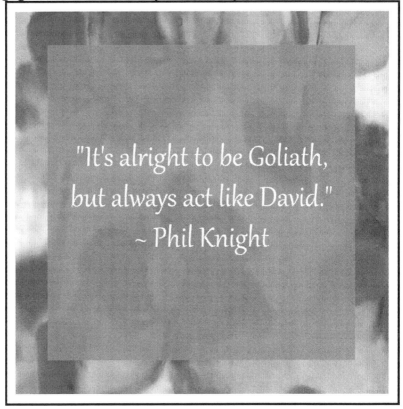

"It's alright to be Goliath, but always act like David."
~ Phil Knight

Likability is more important in video than even in person – and harder to pull off according to *The Likeability Factor* author, Tim Sanders and *Wall Street Journal* columnist Sue Shellenbarger, who offer tips. And virtual communication is increasingly visual. The growing use of videoconferencing and videos for learning, marketing, social engagement and more are making your LQ (LikeAbility Quotient) ever more vital for your success in work and in support of causes and other interests that most matter to you.

• People watching a speaker on a videoconference are more influenced by how much they like the speaker than by the quality of the speaker's arguments, according to a 2008 study in *Management Science Journal*. The opposite is true when a speaker appears in person.

• Likable people are more apt to be hired, get help at work, get useful information from others and have mistakes forgiven.

• Some make a negative impression on video by becoming stiff and emotionless, or by exaggerating their points. Overacting is rampant.

Tip: The "big three" behaviors most important to a speaker's likability on video are making eye contact by looking into the camera, smiling naturally when you talk and varying your tone of voice to convey warmth and enthusiasm, according to Ben Decker of Decker Communications.

Part 2: Mutuality Matters More – The Higher the Tech, the Higher the Touch

Sure, the proliferation of apps is making our lives better in many ways, yet nothing lifts our spirits like feeling the camaraderie you evoke when around others, even strangers, it seems. That experience has no app – just you, in person, making the first move toward connecting.

Early in my work life I was sometimes surprised to see how some people were promoted faster than others who worked harder and seemed more diligent, as I was raised to do. Now I see why this happens. The surprise, for me, was that research shows you are most likely to look trustworthy to others and be liked *if you first exhibit warmth and then competence*, not the reverse. Our Danish family emphasized diligent work; thus competence was most apparent upfront. Yet we are hardwired to respond first to visible warmth from others and can feel coolness in them when they are simply demonstrating competence, even when intending to be helpful.

We most admire those who exude the right balance of strength and warmth, even though the notion runs counter to Machiavelli's famous view that "It is better to be feared than loved if you cannot be both." Like to learn how? If you're a woman or a person of color, this capacity is especially vital, according to *Compelling People* co-authors John Neffinger and Matthew Kohut. Attempting to first show competence can actually cut you off from others, they found. Harvard researcher Amy Cuddy came to the same conclusion and advocate open body styles to visibly demonstrate warmth.

How Do Leaders Rate on the Warmth/Strength Scale?

Enter a well-known person's name in the search box. Then you can rate that public figure's combination of strength and warmth and also see their overall rating.

- *Strength:* Skill and will
- *Warmth:* Shared concerns or interests

Emotions are contagious, especially when we are face-to-face with others rather than virtually. First demonstrate warmth and then competence because "we are highly sensitive to warmth and its absence," according to Chris Malone and Susan T. Fiske, authors of *The Human Brand.* You are judged for your trustworthiness within an eye blink of someone's seeing your face. About two eye blinks later, others decide on your level of competence, according to Janine Willis and Alexander Todorov.

When first meeting or re-meeting people, consider in advance what you most like and admire about each person. Make that thought top-of-mind when you first see them. Also, if your team is meeting with others, or co-presenting, meet in advance to share out loud those traits you admire in those whom you will be seeing. That way you increase the chances of warming them up to you, to your team and to each other. That fuels fueling a virtuous circle of mutually reinforcing good will.

Tip: People are more generous after holding a hot cup of coffee and more callous after holding a cold drink, discovered Yale University psychologist John Bargh. Offer a warm cup of some beverage to those who come to see you. Consider giving each person a hot cup of coffee as they enter the meeting.

Tip: Meeting around a round or, even better, an oval table where everyone can easily see each other boosts feelings of mutual warmth. The opposite happens when meeting around a square table or, worst of all, a long rectangular table. Compound the warmth-sapping effect by meeting in a noisy setting or even where there is ambient noise from an air conditioner or other source.

Those you sit closest to at a meeting or in a workspace are often the ones with whom you feel most comfortable. Consequently:

•   Be aware of this bias and make a point of engaging others who are farther away. If you are a manager, have people change where they sit periodically. Zappos and Downtown Project founder Tony Hsieh actually assigns employees parking spaces in garages that are a block or so away from their offices to spur more opportunities for collisions–serendipitous interactions with people you might not otherwise meet or see as often. That spurs more camaraderie, collaboration and community feelings, he discovered. Also if, as Kio Stark suggests in *Atlantic* magazine, cities can be interaction machines, why can't your workplace or conference?

• Sit next to someone you have not yet met or where you have felt some friction. Sidling – sitting or standing side-by-side with someone – boosts the chances of your getting in sync and thus boosting trust. Walking together compounds that feeling of mutuality. Walking to the meeting together or taking a daily constitutional together can often strengthen your relationship and allow you to accomplish more together, in your personal or work life, more than texting or even sitting in the same room together.

• Meet face to face when you want others to be inspired about your idea. People are three to four times more likely to spread your idea after talking with you in person that after hearing about it online, according to Contagious author Jonah Berger in an interview with Bryan Kramer. Ed Keller and Brad Fay, co-authors of The Face-to-Facebook, heartily agree.

•

Brash Friendliness Pushes Us Back, Yet Warm Geniality Pulls Us In

A warm smile tends to beget a smile in return. Yet an effusive, over-the-top laugh and wide grin, for example, may cause an introvert or someone who has just gone through a trying time to back into their shell. So bring out the friendly, expressive part of you that's close to the energy level of the person you are with. Then you are more likely to close the gap of connection rather than widen it.

Make Your Welcoming Expression a Comforting Gift: Avoid The Screen Face

As we increasingly look down and focus on what's on our phone, our faces tend to look serious or even dour or dismissive. Unfortunately, we often maintain that screen face expression when we look up to engage with others. Since behaviors create moods and moods are contagious, we are setting up an unfriendly frame for the rest of the interaction.

Tip: Adopt the Golden Golden Rule. Treat others *as they want to be treated* rather than as you want to be treated, which is our first instinct.

Foster Feelings of Companionate Love at Work

Companies that foster feelings of mutuality, or companionate love, reduce employees' withdrawal from work, according to Wharton management professor Sigal Barsade and George Mason assistant professor Mandy O'Neill, who found that this feeling also led to higher levels of employee engagement with their work via greater teamwork and employee satisfaction.

It happens when colleagues who are together day in and day out ask and care about each other's work and even non-work issues. They are careful of each other's feelings. They show compassion when things don't go well. And they also show affection and caring — which can be bringing somebody a cup of coffee when you go get your own or just listening when a co-worker needs to talk, Mason, Barsade and O'Neill discovered.

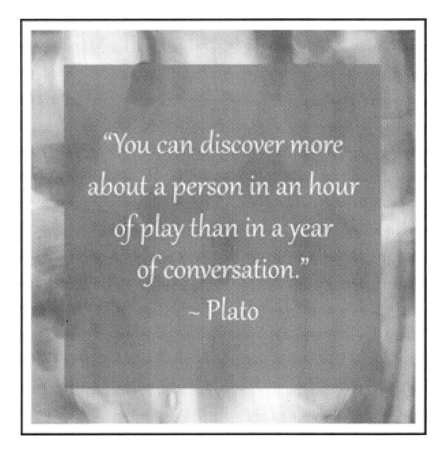

"You can discover more about a person in an hour of play than in a year of conversation."
~ Plato

Shared In-Person Experiences Are Play, Spending, Loyalty And Learning

What do the New England Patriots rabid fans' active-sharing mid-game comments via immersive Wi-Fi have in common with Peabody Hotel guests'
avid videoing and picture-snapping of the daily duck walk? Or parents standing in front of a large store wall of bewildering choices in children's car seats, looking down at their free Car Seat Helper app from Phoenix Children's Hospital, comforted in knowing they'll be able to make a wise choice about their child's safety?

Spur Public Sharing to Solidify Connections, Centered Around What You Offer

Each of those situations spurs positive, shared experiences, shaped by organizations that seek to serve people better at the right time and in helpful ways. From the Gillette Stadium's pervasive Wi Fi to support fans' sharing to hotels' storyboarding scenes to envelop guests, people-serving business managers increasingly recognize the power and need to boost involvement, loyalty and bragging rights to make people feel closer in the experience they offer. Mutuality matters. Instilling bragging rights is dubbed *The Ultimate Moment of Truth* by Brian Solis in his next book, *What's the Future of Business?* It represents the experience people share after using your product and engaging with your company over time. Blog posts, YouTube videos, reviews – each in its own way – spur people to take next steps.

Experience Together Participation-Play-Evoking Public Architecture

Like Cloud Gate ("the bean" in Chicago), some public art is designed to foster closeness and play, even among strangers. Others evoke collective awe and solemnity, like the Vietnam Memorial. Others get us in sync, literally walking together, like the High Line in New York City. With New York's High Line heading toward the completion of its celebrated reuse of an abandoned elevated railroad, followers of parks and public space are wondering what's next. Friends of the High Line co-founder Robert Hammond, is planning an epic geographical mutuality: bring the High Line across the Hudson and eventually across America.

Tip: Construct a High Line, central plaza or mini-park in your community, where we feel comfortable gathering, preferably outdoors. Boost what Downtown Project founder Tony Hsieh dubs collisions that create camaraderie, serendipity and mutuality: With friends and strangers, let's walk and sit face to face more often in interesting places. Be a placemaker?

Go Fishing for Closer Conversations

"I swear, my dear. Sometimes our conversations remind me of a broken sword. She raised an eyebrow. Sharp as hell, he said, but lacking a point," wrote **Brandon Sanderson** in *Warbreaker*. Until you find the lure and the hook on which someone will bite, you won't pull them closer. You are talking to yourself. Soon they may show irritation or go on a mental vacation. "It is all right to hold a conversation but you should let go of it now and then." ~Richard Armour

Go Slow to Go Fast in Growing a Stronger Bond With Others

When you see someone's interest rise in the conversation, you have a glimpse of the hook that can best connect you together. Ask follow up questions, directly related to what that person just said. If you do just this much, recent research shows you are among the five percent of Americans in conversation.

In so doing, you accomplish two things. You've increased their openness and warmth toward you, because you've demonstrated you care. And you've had a closer look at the hook that most matters to them in the conversation. Now you can speak to their hottest interest, in a way that can serve you both.

Listening is a magnetic and strange thing, a creative force. The friends who listen to us are the ones we move toward. When we are listened to, it creates us, makes us unfold and expand. ~Karl Menninger

First Focus On Making Them Feel Great

One of the biggest misconceptions about connecting is seeking, first, to be liked. The counterintuitive way to get someone to like you is in knowing this core truth: If they like the way they feel when around you, they will like you. In fact, they will project onto you the character traits they most like in others, even if you have not yet exhibited them.

Conversely, if they do not like the way they act when around you, they will instinctively blame you for it, regardless of the true reason. They will project onto you some of the qualities they most dislike in others. What's worse, they will go out of their way to prove they are right, even in ways that damage their reputation as well as yours.

The true spirit of conversation consists in building on another man's observation, not overturning it. ~Edward G. Bulwer-Lytton

Eleven More Ways to Connect Better in Conversation And Stay Sought-After

Both online and in person, connective conversation is increasingly rare, so your capacity to connect deeply with diverse individuals will cause you to stand out and attract smarter support sooner in all parts of your life. Here are more pointers to support that habit:

1.   Be direct in answering questions. First answer. Then elaborate, not the reverse, which is increasingly common. Don't give qualifiers and background before answering. That's underbrush he must wade through. You may seem to be going off on a tangent rather than responding to him or, worse yet, being evasive.

2.   Focus on what she is saying right now. Avoid trying to anticipate what she is going to say. You may miss what she actually means.

To truly listen is to risk being changed forever. ~Sakej Henderson

3.   Don't interrupt. It sends the message that your views are more important than his.

4.   Confirm your understanding of what she said, using her words. Don't paraphrase. You are keeping a thread to the conversation and thus moving you both forward in it.

Every moment counts, and moments are lost when you're not in them 100 percent. ~Tachi Yamada, M.D.

5.   Ask follow-up questions to clarify and to glean the specific benefits he seeks or problem he wants to solve – or other conscious or unconscious desire he has in the conversation.

6.   Take notes. It demonstrates interest and respect and enables you to recall exactly what was said. When you take notes, you triple the amount you remember – even if you never look at those notes again.

7.   Control outside interruptions and distractions. Where possible, meet in a place that is not noisy, where seats are comfortable.

8.   Sit at a right angle, sidling, rather than across from her. We tend to like each other better when walking, sitting or standing side by side or at right angles from each other.

9.   Avoid patterned shirts, blouses or other distractive clothing, especially on the upper half of your body. Patterns, like noises, shorten attention spans.

It was impossible to get a conversation going, everybody was talking too much. ~Yogi Berra

10.   Lean slightly forward toward him and look directly at him much of the time. Nod sometimes and do not fidget. Just as smiling actually lifts your mood as well as those who see it, acting interested in these ways often makes you feel more interested.

11.   Remain genial and receptive. Do not react negatively, even and especially to highly charged words and tones. Hear her out. Then respond. Say, for example, "May I tell you my thoughts on that?" Don't change the topic. Some people will cool down and begin to talk calmly once they vent their anger and frustrations and feel heard.

The Icing On The Cake Of These Conversation Cues

The more strongly someone connects with you, the more likely it is that they will emulate your becoming behavior, tell others about your positive traits and actions, and want to introduce you to opportunities, colleagues, friends and the friends of their friends. Sound like a way to savor your life with others? For further ideas on fostering convivial, worthwhile conversation, I recommend *Crucial Conversations*, *Conversational Intelligence*, *Difficult Conversations* and *Fierce Conversations*.

Listening is a magnetic and strange thing, a creative force. The friends who listen to us are the ones we move toward. When we are listened to, it creates us, makes us unfold and expand. ~Karl Menninger

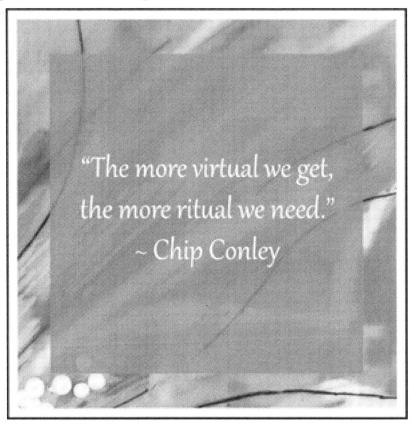

"The more virtual we get, the more ritual we need."
~ Chip Conley

Nudge Us to Do Better Together

As the invisible gorilla test famously proved, we are sometimes blind to what's happening right in front of our eyes, especially if we are focused on a specific task or other interest. Ironically that means you can direct others' attention in certain ways, thus nudging them toward taking action that is better for them and/or others, or worse. Consider how to adapt these nudges to situations that matter to you.

Make the Right Option More Fun for Us

• After an image of a housefly was etched inside the urinals at Amsterdam's Schiphol airport, the amount of misdirected urine fell by about 80 percent, according to the airport. They had something at which to aim.

• To sway people to get more exercise by taking the stairs instead of an elevator or escalator, one inventive group made the stairs sunnier and another group made climbing the stairs a musical adventure we could share. Here are more ways to make stairs the more compelling choice.

• To get more of your friends to vote for your favorite candidate, add your photo to the appeal you send to your friends via social channels, discovered *Connected* co-author James Fowler.

• Suggest the positive benefit rather than citing the negative. More people are likely to buy meat described as "75 percent lean beef" than "25 percent fat."

• Toss in the first rewards when offering a loyalty card. Many more people came back to car wash and came back more often when they were gifted two free stamps on their loyalty card that offered "buy eight car washes, and get your ninth one free" than those who were not given those freebies upfront. This Endowed Progress Effect builds in the artificial sense that they are already on their way to the goal, so recipients are more persistent in reaching it.

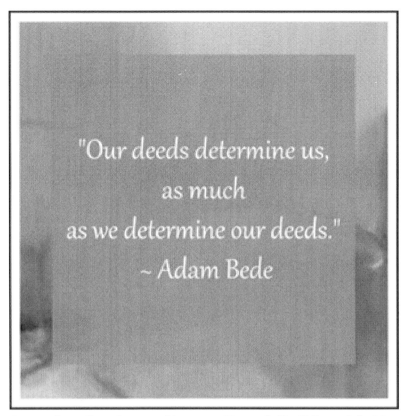

"Our deeds determine us,
as much
as we determine our deeds."
~ Adam Bede

Appeal to Our Better Nature, Especially When it's Not on Display

Instead of attempting to guilt-trip motorists to stop throwing trash out their car windows with "Don't Litter" signs, the state of Texas had much greater success by appealing to Texans' pride, with signage declaring "Don't mess with Texas."

Make It Easier to Do the Right Thing

If you worked for an organization that offered automatic payroll deduction for savings, you'd be much more likely to save if the system was one where you had to opt-out of the savings option rather than needing to opt in to do so.

Give Us an Obvious Sign

When you see a path of big green footprints, you are more likely to follow them to the public bins and throw your trash away. That's what the Danish Nudging Network discovered. First they gave distinctively wrapped caramel candies to pedestrians in an area. Afterwards they searched nearby garbage cans, bicycle baskets and even ashtrays for the empty wrappers, and counted them. Then they painted green footprints up to recycling bins and repeated the experiment. While 70% of the wrappers weren't found in both settings, 46% fewer wrappers were littered in the "green footprints" experiment.

What symbolic scene, path or interactive object can you use to nudge others to act better? "What's most likely to sway us isn't the most potent or familiar or instructive aspect of a situation; but most prominent in our consciousness at the time," discovered *Influence* author Robert Cialdini.

Tip: Make it easier, faster and/or more fun, convenient to do the right thing with and/or for others. Plus provide bragging rights, such as an enticing backdrop or other scene where they'll want to take a selfie with others to share.

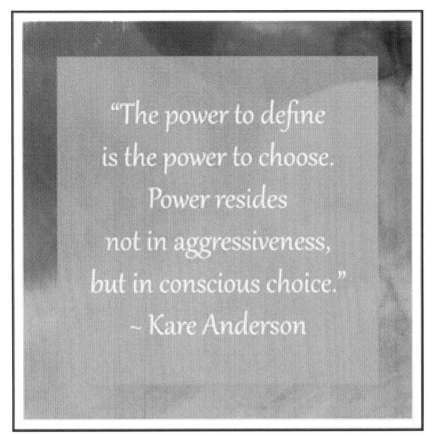

"The power to define
is the power to choose.
Power resides
not in aggressiveness,
but in conscious choice."
~ Kare Anderson

When We Visibly Do Something Together, Others Are More Likely to Follow

What Robert Cialdini dubbed "social proof" is a powerful way to attract involvement or other support. When we think we're out of step with our peers, "the part of our brain that registers pain shifts into overdrive," according to Cialdini. Our herd instinct is strong.

The effect is strongest in situations of uncertainty (individuals are unsure and/or the situation is ambiguous) or similarity (we are most likely to follow people who are *like* us).

Here are some examples:

- You choose the busy restaurant rather than the nearby empty one. You're attracted to the crowded booths at the fair or tradeshow.

- After a murder/suicide is heavily reported, head-on car collisions and airplane crashes immediately go up.

- Fewer people now smoke in the United States, as it became uncool to do so except in clusters where it's still popular.

- For twenty minutes a day, kids who were afraid of dogs were set in front of a boy playing happily with a dog. After only four days, 67 percent of them climbed into a playpen with a dog and played with him. Shy kids can be helped too.

- If several people around you are overweight, you are more likely to gain pounds.

- Bartenders sometimes "salt" the tip jar to get patrons to drop in money.

- Desperate women invade the men's restroom at a Springsteen concert – only after the first one or two bravely entered.

- One business attracts more customers because, unlike competitors, it displays testimonials.

When you see a woman looking at one of two men, you presume he is more attractive and important than the other man, simply because of where she is looking.

Tip: Display your product near complementary, noncompeting and popular products or other objects.

Pull Us Towards Wanting It Too
Help Others Become the Stars in Their Situation

Imagine the astonishment of the staff, including the sommelier, at Bone's, an Atlanta steak house, when they started handing dining guests iPads at the table, loaded with a copy of the wine list. Purchases of wine shot up 11 percent. Mused Mr. Reno, the sommelier, "With the information on the device, they seem more apt to experiment by buying a different varietal or going outside their price range. It stuns me, but they seem to trust the device more than they trust me, and these are people I've waited on for ten years." Or, perhaps diners feel more comfortable and confident looking at various wines themselves and discussing them at the table. That fuels their feelings of mutuality.

Hint: Let others take charge of your message, tweak it for their needs, look good in front of others and thus sell themselves on it.

Tip: People are more likely to buy your idea or product if you provide ways for them to be visible, valued experts. Enable them to gain bragging rights – especially in front of others who matter to them.

Spark The Emotions That Spur Us To Share Your Message

This headline, "Exec loses job after allegedly slapping toddler on plane," is an anger-evoking true story that spread quickly. Understanding why can help you spread your ideas, piggybacking on certain kinds of events. "High arousal" negative emotions such as anger or anxiety spur us to share messages with others, discovered Wharton professor Jonah Berger, author of *Contagious*.

So do certain high-arousal positive emotions: awe, excitement and amusement or humor. Susan Boyle's unexpected singing performance, for example, evoked awe and

100 million views within nine days. Even years later, she inked a movie deal. *Les Miserables'* movie producer Cameron Mackintosh said her success reinforced his interest in making that movie.

Evoke Pride and Other High-Arousal Emotions

Evoking pride or righteous anger also spurs sharing, according to *Scaling Up Excellence* co-authors an dStanford professors Bob Sutton and Huggy Rao, because "such feelings make people feel powerful and in control of the world around them, which in turn triggers assertive and confident action."

Evoking pride instead of shame made a success of the anti-littering campaign "Don't mess with Texas." To get Stanford soccer players to agree to wear helmets, fellow students littered their field with smashed watermelons and then created and posted photoshopped images around the field of unprotected heads of soccer players next to the watermelons.

Warning: Some Emotions Stifle Our Desire to Share

Not all positive emotions actually motivate us to share ideas with others, Berger discovered. "Low-arousal" positive emotions in response to a message, such as contentment, don't spur us to share.

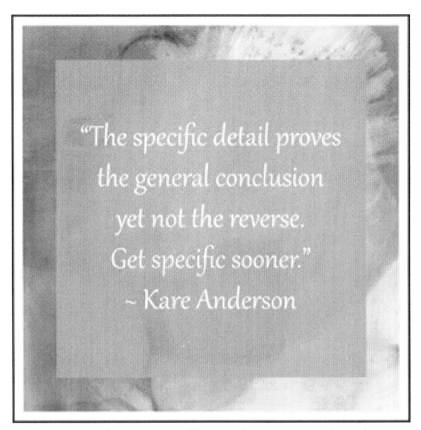

"The specific detail proves the general conclusion yet not the reverse. Get specific sooner."
~ Kare Anderson

Tie Your Product to Familiar and Frequent Situations

Even citing mutuality between products can help see yours. For example, "Kit Kat and coffee break" can sound like a rather bland brand slogan. Yet sales skyrocketed. Why? Because the company tied its ad campaign to a frequent habit for many people: drinking coffee. Those who see the message, or its offshoots, may be triggered to think about eating a Kit Kat candy bar whenever they take a coffee break. Conversely, GEICO's attention-grabbing TV ads suggesting that switching over to their auto insurance was so simple that even a caveman could do it were not as successful. As *Contagious* author Jonah Berger points out, "We don't see many cavemen in our daily lives. The advertisement is unlikely to come to mind as often, making it less likely to be talked about."

Tip: Connect your message to a situation that your kind of customer frequently experiences so it triggers them to think of your product whenever they are in that situation.

Danger: Don't Do This. Translation: But Many Others Are

Some widely visible "anti" campaigns that attempt to stop certain behaviors, such as kids using drugs, instead evoke the opposite reaction because they give the habit more visibility, thus social currency. Public service announcements that warn of such dangers actually serve as "social proof" that many people appear to be doing it, so it must be okay, thus encouraging young people to use marijuana.

Focus on Real-Life Exposure to Transport Your Message

Most people believe that at least 50 percent of word-of-mouth messages happen online. "The actual number is seven percent," writes Berger, citing **Keller Fay Group** research. That may be because "it is easier to see," adds Berger. "Social media sites provide a handy record of all the clips, comments, and other content we share online. But we don't think as much about all the offline conversation we had over the same time period because we can't actually see them."

Create In-Person Experiences That Many Can Socially Share

Here are two real-life success stories to spur your thinking:

1.   Honest Tea launched an eye-catching, offline "experiment" in several U.S. cities, linking their unusual brand name to the action of consumers choosing the bottle with the flavor they most wanted. In turn, they tied both to two familiar triggers: city sidewalks and store shelves. They thus created a real-life multiple-story generator, with consumers as the actors in it capturing our voyeuristic interest in other people's honesty. Each incident in each experiment became a vessel to carry a story that featured all kinds of people picking up

Honest Tea bottles, imprinting that action in the viewers' minds. Here's the experiment: The company created unstaffed, pop-up sidewalk stands where passersby could pick up as many bottles as they wanted — and pay by the honor system. People anywhere in the world could watch how people responded to the tempting opportunity to cheat.

That's because of live video-streaming coverage via hidden cameras in the cities where the experiment was held. Quirky, admittedly unscientific story angles abounded that the media loved to cover. What city has the most honest people? Are blondes more honest than bald people?

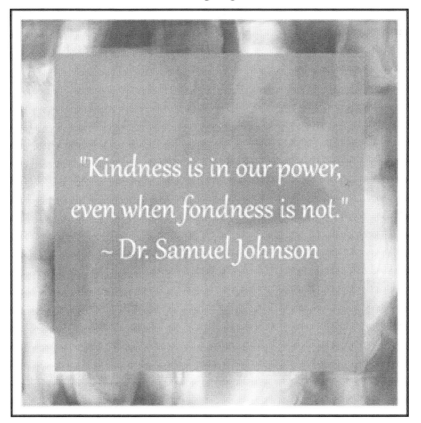

"Kindness is in our power, even when fondness is not."
~ Dr. Samuel Johnson

2. While most junk mail is thrown away without ever being opened, a mailer for Bulk Cat Litter Warehouse drew the attention of its target market. The firm added catnip concentrate to its mailers, which made the cats go wild about

them. Plus, of course, they attracted considerable media coverage.

How Your Emotional Story Can Carry Benefits You Want Them to Feel and Act On

Peel away the layers of the onion, meaning the factually stated features a company often cites to sell something. Look for the underlying emotional need or desire people could have for your product so you can start the conversation about them. Craft a story to wrap around that desire so we get an emotional experience of using the benefits you want to tout. That's why Google Creative Labs member Anthony Cafaro resisted creating the usual pithy and factual description. Instead, he concocted a romance story, Parisian Love. We get pulled into the unfolding romance, voyeuristically watching the search unfold as the characters use the tools the project was supposed to tout. They represented the expanded functionality in Google's new search interface. "Features like finding flights, autocorrect, and language translation," cites Berger, who goes on to describe how the story unfolds and triggers us to share.

Imprint Your Idea On Us Via a Visual Framework

To instantly imprint your key concept on others' minds, create a visual representation of it, recommends Denise Brosseau, in *Ready to Be a Thought Leader?* For greater impact, alter an already famous visual framework to display your core idea. For example, in his book *Peak: How Great Companies Get Their Mojo from Maslow*, Chip Conley, founder of Joie de Vivre Hospitality, altered Maslow's familiar pyramid that shows humans' Hierarchy of Needs. He simplified the pyramid to show three layers of needs of employees, clients and investors. Create even more memorability by labeling your ideas as Conley did. He named those three increasingly meaningful stages for connecting more deeply with customers, the book's main message. Plus he attached pithy one to two word benefit statements to each label.

For another visual diagram of a concept, see Charles H. Green's Trust Quotient. Alternatively, create a picture that memorably captures your core idea as these book covers do: *Stumbling on Happiness*, Stressaholic and *Connected.* Discover more ways to make your message indelible and shareable via visuals by reading *The Power of Visual Storytelling: How to Use Visuals, Videos, and Social Media to Market Your Brand* by Ekaterina Walter and Jessica Gioglio.

Also consider magnifying the memorability of your core idea by creating a word for it as *Stressaholic* author Heidi Hanna managed to do. Sam Horn shows you how in *POP!: Create the Perfect Pitch, Title, and Tagline for Anything*

Instill Bragging Rights That Boost Participation and Sharing

"I love Southwest! #SWA," wrote China Gorman on Facebook. "The pilot of our flight to Orlando just approached [people] sitting next to me with two extreme special-needs boys (4 and 6 years old) to ask if the boys wanted to board first and get their pictures taken in the cockpit before everyone else boards. The pilot was just walking through the boarding area, noticed the family and asked. Really. One of the many reasons I give Southwest my corporate and personal business."

On the popular site TLNT, Ron Thomas shared her comments, adding his praise and thus attracting more praise and stories from others about their positive experiences with Southwest and other companies.

Your instinctively empathic, sometimes unexpected actions of support for others not only lifts your mood but also elevate the mood of those that witness the actions or hear about them. You instill bragging rights in others, reinforcing the depth of their loyalty and the vivid credibility of their characterizations as they share the story with others. In so doing you also strengthen their sense of mutuality with you. Get ideas on how to surprise and delight customers from T. Scott Gross' classic, *Positively Outrageous Customer Service*.

Tip: Create or find popular #hashtags to boost others' sharing, suggests Kim Garst.

Creating the "Hook" Enables Others to Earn Bragging Rights by Hanging On It

When Matthew May offered a book with a very concrete concept, the *Laws of Subtraction* (six smart laws to simplify work and life), he created what Frans Johansson dubs a "hook" on which we can hang our ideas related to his book..

As we participate with others, we all learn more, faster, around those core concepts and feeling closer. Plus, by participating, we boost May's visibility value, and ours. Just like building equity in the home you own, creating a hook that pulls in others creates greater equity or value for your brand. It begins by instilling the opportunity for others to gain bragging rights by contributing.

Create a meaningful, memorable and pithy set of core truths that attract participation. Examples that have been widely shared and adapted: Stephen Covey's *7 Habits of Highly Effective People*, Gretchen Rubin's 8 Splendid Truths.

Tip: Design a site that acts as a hook for bragging rights, such as **Anita Campbell's BizSugar**, where the most popular ideas from others gain the most visibility. Also see **Guy Kawasaki's AllTop**, where the most popular blog posts, by topic, rise to the top of visibility.

Share the Story Others Want to Be In

Peter Guber's advice, in *Tell to Win*, shows how stories can build in bragging rights by creating **purposeful narratives**. Then you can **pull others into your story** because they can see a role they want to play in that purpose. In their re-telling of your story, they reshape it, making it theirs, more multifaceted and thus more relevant to more kinds of people the more it is shared. Certainly that expanding, pass-along effect can create value for any kind of organization.

Tip: Multiply the ways and reduce the steps it takes for others to share your idea, offer or story. For example, *Huffington Post* launched a **Third Metric** section to cover diverse examples of "redefining success beyond money and power" from "Sue Parks: Why Exercise Is a Great Way to Boost Your Bottom Line" to Why This Banker Quit Wall Street to Become a Monk" and "Improve Your Life by Improving the Lives of Others."

By hosting a conference on the theme, they provided another way for people to bond around the topic and "brag" about their favorite stories face to face.

Craft "Top" or "Best" Lists Related to Your Core Expertise

Fifty people, including me, were spurred to cite Cheryl K. Burgess and Tom Pick's annual Nifty50 award honoring women writers on Twitter for the unsurprising reason: we were on the list. Extreme Networks' CMO, Vala Afshar, has made a brand-boosting art of creating such lists. They evoke the Coattail Effect (not "just" politicians want to ride others' coattails to fame) and Ripple Effect, where word ripples out as friends and colleagues of those on the list demonstrate their support and desire to be part of the reflected glow of visibility by sharing the news.

Tip: Turn your list into a badge, Instagram, Pinterest or Infographic and perhaps even cite it in a short Vine, KlabLab Stitch and/or Gloopt video.

Create Adventures That Make Employee Heroes and Customers Smile

WestJet brightens and improves lives of customers, employees and others, not just at Christmas with this "miracle" unfolding event watched by 1.57 million, but in several ways over the years, including helping those in Haiti via a partnership with the practical nonprofit Live Different. Why don't more companies create such unexpected adventures for people to feel, in-person together?

Create public sculpture like CloudGate or a gathering place like High Line or a commemorative site like the Vietnam Veterans Memorial in Washington, D.C., and in Portland, OR, which pulls us literally into action, sometimes feeling closer around a connective mood such as playfulness, awe or reverence.

Imagine walking into a hote lobby and seeing a kinetic chandelier that turns guests' movements and social media updates into a light show. That bragging-rights-generating experience was created as a result of Chip Conley's team collaborating with IDEO and interior designer Colum McCartan in the design of The Epiphany hotel in Palo Alto, aptly in the heart of Silicon Valley. This "Edison"-style chandelier stirs mutuality in hotel guests as an opportunity to observe and discuss it in the lobby as they photobomb it to share with friends. Plus, it's attracted wide publicity for the hotel.

Yet you can accomplish some of the same mutuality-building effects in your physical space in low-tech ways. Imagine having large glass bowls at pausing areas in your semi-public place, whether it's a hotel, hospital, store or stadium. In each bowl, place fortune-cookie-paper-sized colored sheets with sayings that are relevant for your kind of place, with signage in and around the bowl inviting people to take one out and contribute their own sayings by filling out a blank sheet and putting it in the bowl. Of course, you have to prepare for the inappropriate contributions, yet the upside of spurring connective conversations on the spot may be worth it.

• Host a crowd-attracting experiment that is relevant to your brand, and create legs to the story so it lasts longer, attracts media coverage and scales involvement. That's what Honest Tea achieved when they set up self-service (honesty-based) kiosks in 30 U.S. cities, where people could get a bottle of Honest Tea, with their behavior video-streamed live.

Tip: In signage, share a significant, specific and moving detail that can set the stage for others' experience. For example, I wish a sign were incorporated into the Vietnam Veterans' Memorial saying something like, "Of the 58,286 soldiers we honor here, more than half were under 22 when they died for our country's freedom."

• Domino's Pizza instigated a mutuality-centric turnaround with a "warts and all" transparency, allowing customers to watch their pizza being made and easily say what they think of their pizza via an online tracker. And by swearing off food styling, showing their pizzas as they really look. Show you care, like a good mother.

• Curalate's Fanreel enables companies to gather and place user-generated images onto their websites and product pages. Urban Outfitters uses it to pull a feed from Instagrams of images with the hashtag UOONYOU and puts the best images on its site. It also made the images shoppable, so a customer who likes another customer's look in a photo can immediately buy the clothing. All these socially visible actions spur bragging rights from buyers. You can also pull relevant pictures from Pinterest and Tumblr to curate on your site and invite current and prospective customers to help each other find stuff they like, thus evoking the magnetic power of social proof.

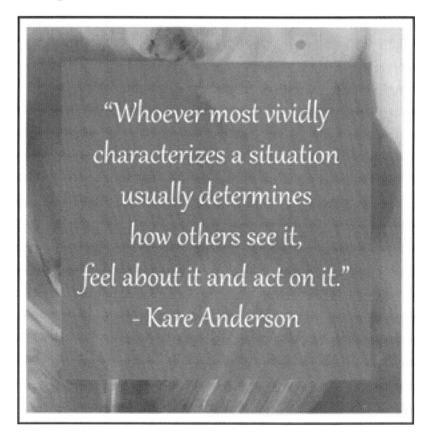

"Whoever most vividly characterizes a situation usually determines how others see it, feel about it and act on it."
- Kare Anderson

Piggyback On a Big, Trending Story

Just as runners who are already running can pull ahead of those who have not yet started, it's easier to gain ground over others by jumping on an already trending story. Just be sure your offer is relevant, quick, simple and a fun way others can feel good participating. The best piggybacking methods enable us to customize and share something. That's what *Slate magazine* quickly did. After John Travolta mangled Idina Menzel's name at the Oscars, *Slate* seized the opportunity to let you Travoltify your name. Mine? Kobe Andrenson. Want to find yours out right now? See how enticingly simple that suggestion is? How could you evoke a positive emotion. For example, Slate's widget helped us have fun with others *and to be funny together*.

Tip: Label yourself or your ideas before someone else does it in a way you don't like. Whoever most vividly characterizes a situation usually determines how others see it in their mind's eye, discuss it and act on it.

Lucky Menzel got priceless visibility to a wider audience because of Travolta's verbal stumble. She probably could have generated even more visibility if she had offered a way for others to engage with her right after the Oscars. For example, she could have collaborated with a songwriting friend to create a sweet, short verse she could sing, thanking Travolta, drolly pronouncing his name correctly, and inviting others to finish the final sentence of her song with their own sentiment, digitally added via a widget and shared.

One clever piggybacking action, covered by *Los Angeles Times*' David Ng, is this joke circulating on Twitter: "A fake playbill notice for the Broadway musical 'If/Then' states that its star, Idina Menzel, will be replaced by her alter-ego, Adele Dazeem."

Position Your Idea or Product Where Receptivity Is Likely To Be High

Sure, famous, well-liked celebrities like Ellen DeGeneres can usually get others engaged in something they do. Yet, referencing the famous computer simulations conducted by Duncan Watts and Peter Dodds, *The Leap* author Rick Smith suggests that the most frequent way something spreads "is not by a few influentials but their polar opposite: a 'critical mass of influenced people, each of whom adopts, say, a look or a brand after being exposed by a single adopting neighbor.'" Concludes Smith, "It is not necessarily the source of the idea, but people's degree of receptivity to it that matters most."

An example: Rather than going door to door or standing outside a grocery store, Girl Scout Danielle Lei set her cookie table up on the sidewalk just outside a marijuana clinic in San Francisco, selling 117 boxes in two hours.

Talk about selling where receptivity is likely to be, well, high. Being involved in a "first ever" action is sometimes likely to be provocative yet also most likely to be widely quoted.

Turn Your Concept Into A Visual Framework You Own

Not that she needs to, but DeGeneres can't own the Twitter image she orchestrated. Yet you can own the image of your concept. To instantly imprint in others' minds your key concept, create a visual representation of it, recommends Denise Brosseau in *Ready to Be a Thought Leader?* For greater impact, alter an already famous visual framework to fit your core idea. Brosseau cites Chip Conley's memorable simplification of the ascending categories in Maslow's Hierarchy of Needs into the three core themes of his book *PEAK*. Conley not only labeled the three increasingly meaningful categories for connecting more deeply with customers – the book's main message – but also attached a one- or two-word benefit to each stage of greater customer connection.

How To Own Your Distinctive Concept

Whether you are crafting a book, campaign, course or other use for your concept, you can and should own it as intellectual property, recommends Brosseau, who elaborates on these steps in her book:

1. Create a simple, preferably visual, representation that is easy to understand.
2. Clearly document how to use that framework.
3. Give it a great name.
4. Show proof that it works.
5. Protect and control its use.

What specific methods have you discovered to spur others to share your idea or buy your product or support your cause?

Adapt Other Successful Share Methods to Your Situation

For other productive and proven ways to share, see Shareable, Crowd Companies, Mesh and Collaborative Consumption.

Just as Jeremiah Owyang suggests for companies, that "sharing is the new buying" in the collaborative economy, sharing for individuals is vital in this increasingly connected yet complex world.

And for both organizations and individuals, forms of sharing are most successful when they are based on a mutual mindset where we who participate see an obvious shared benefit.

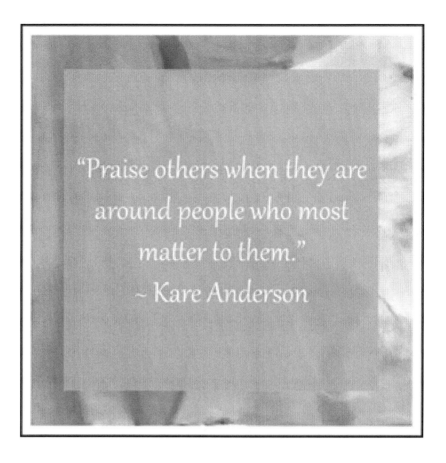

"Praise others when they are around people who most matter to them."
~ Kare Anderson

Cultivate An Us Attitude For Us
Create Convivial and Productive Teams

What's the secret to keeping close-knit relationships in organizations as different as Gore, Saddleback Church and TEDx organizers? It's simple yet surprisingly rare. Participants work in one or more small groups or teams that are networked within the larger organization. Such an approach appeals to the universal desire for meaningful work, progress, recognition and a sense of belonging. Few organizations are structured this way, despite ample proof that it is the best way to optimize talent and innovation.

Tip: We are most likely to stay highly engaged and happy in organizations that:

- Operate as small groups that are tight-knit, cross-functional and sometimes self-organized.

- Have enough rules (carrots and sticks) and structure to enable us to use best talents together on meaningful work.

- Encourage us to propose mutually beneficial changes in those rules and structure.

- Spur our shared learning, camaraderie and mutual support.

Acknowledging Negative Emotions Is Worthwhile

The creator of Wharton's popular "Success Course," G. Richard Shell notes, "When it comes to gaining wisdom, negative emotions have a place of honor right next to positive ones. The price of enlightenment seems to be suffering, not smiling." Since anyone radically different from you inevitably won't act right (like you), you get a priceless opportunity to see your biggest hot buttons as you react. You can practice turning moments of potential miscommunication or friction into opportunities to speak to each other's good intent — and feel the satisfaction of "doing what you should be doing."

Tip: When you most want to smash someone in the face or flee the room, remember this irony. Cooling off someone's anger can actually draw that person closer to you. See five ways to keep your cool when under fire.

Experience The Freedom of Agreed-Upon Constraints

Be part of a regular tribe that is both bounded and unbounded. That means they have agreed-upon ground rules, from the structure of their meetings to the explicit, mutually beneficial ways they share and collaborate. Yet they are also able to experiment, learn faster from each other, propose changes in how they operate and evolve. Such groups are as diverse as Quantified Self, Rotary International, Y Combinator and Mastermind groups. "In a world of constant flux where our skill sets have a shorter life," we can thrive as we hone our capacity for flexibility and play in situations that are both bounded and unbounded, according to *A New Culture of Learning* co-authors John Seely Brown and Douglas Thomas.

Nimble Teams Rarely Have More Than Seven Members

To reduce stress and confusion in battle, "fire teams" – the basic Marine combat fighting unit – shrunk from twelve to four during World War II, according to James H. Webb. Navy Seals learned, through hard experience, that four-person combat teams perform best. The Roman army had eight guys to a fighting unit, "the number that could fit into a tent," notes former Twitter Engineering SVP Chris Fry, who also found that leaders who have too many teams to form become bottlenecks. McKinsey's consulting teams have one engagement manager and three other members. News aggregator app, Pulse News, discovered that misunderstandings and friction flared as they grew to just eight members and until they divided into three teams. Even average U.S. restaurant reservations are for a party of four. "Less is best," believes Intuit CEO Brad Smith.

"Big teams suck," writes Stanford business professor Bob Sutton. "Seven is a 'magical number' because people can only hold 'seven, plus or minus two' numbers in short-term memory," according to psychologist George Miller.

For most tasks, "four to six members is the best team size," suggests Sutton, citing the research of J. Richard Hackman, who spent nearly 50 years studying team performance:

"Interpersonal friction increases exponentially as team size increases. "As a group expands further, each member devotes more time to coordination chores and less on doing the work." Create pods or teams of four to seven members in your organization and encourage people to be on more than one team. Keep teams together for at least six months and "ideally a year or more," says Fry, "so they can optimize and extend their capabilities."

That's where the power of maximum mutuality kicks in. See Five SmartTribe Accelerators to keep your team on a successful path.

To boost your motivation to organize small groups, know this: We seem more attractive in a group than we do apart. That's the Cheerleader Effect.

Tip: Even surrounded by social networks, we still put the most effort into communicating within small circles.

"Peers can be the best teachers, because they're the ones that remember what it's like to not understand." ~ Peter Norvig

Three Keys to Team Success, Via Wisdom of Crowds, by James Surowiecki:

1. A team's diversity is more important than individual ability.
2. Freedom to disagree is more important than consensus.
3. The voting policies and selection mechanisms you choose as a team are more important than the coherence or even the comprehensibility about what you do.

Tip: As a leader, if you want your team to become higher performing and happier together the best thing you can do is model the behavior that peer mutual accountability matters.

Hint: Your proof that you've succeeded is in how little you need to speak in the meeting. See *Crucial Conversations* author Joseph Grenny's concrete tips for making this transition.

Pair Up to Cut Down Silos and to Scale Performance

"For one week, two people sit together at a computer and work on a major assignment at the same time. The pairs switch every week." Per Sam McNerney, that's how Menlo Innovations' CEO Rich Sheridan overcomes what he dubs the 'Towers of Knowledge' problem, where knowledge is siloed and skills are not redundant.

Tip: Adapt project pairing in your business, membership group or other organization to:

- Facilitate cross-training in a fast, fun way.
- Enable people in different parts of the organization to get to know more people in meaningful ways.
- Enable individuals to learn how to train newcomers.
- Prevent the organization from being hamstrung when one expert leaves.
- Cultivate collaboration, camaraderie, capacity to work through stress and friction, and opportunities for more ideas to bubble up as individuals mix it up more often via pairing.
-

How Musical Chairs Can Foster Mutuality

At the evolving Downtown Project in Las Vegas, Tony Hsieh purposefully assigns parking spaces that are at least a block from where employees work to spur "collisions," meaning serendipitous meetings between individuals. Also, some startups and technology firms are periodically moving employees around so they sit next to different people.

Why? Well, "A worker's immediate neighbors account for 40 percent to 60 percent of every interaction that worker has during the workday, from face-to-face chats to e-mail messages. There's only a 5 percent to 10 percent chance employees are interacting with someone two rows away," according to Ben Waber of Sociometric Solutions.

His firm uses sensors to analyze interaction patterns at work. Waber concludes, "If I keep the org chart the same but change where you sit, it is going to massively change everything." See what happened at Kayak, Hubspot and other firms that played musical chairs. "Grouping workers by department can foster focus and efficiency," discovered MIT's Christian Catalini, yet "mixing them up can lead to experimentation and the potential for breakthrough ideas."

"The community stagnates without the impulse of the individual. The impulse dies away without the sympathy of the community." ~ William James

Bungee Into Productively Engaging With Others

It costs companies one-fifth of an employee's annual salary to replace a worker who leaves, according to a 2012 study by the Center for American Progress think tank.

Tip: To foster retention and happy involvement in paid or volunteer work, arrange for people to collaborate in small groups, and periodically switch groups and their roles within them. That way they explore new sides of one another and "keep partnerships fresh like a healthy marriage, discovered Stanford sociologist Daniel McFarland, who found a second benefit: rotating leadership roles helps everyone involved learn new skills.

Adopt the Low-Cost Way of Learning Better Together

Google encourages employees to take "bungee" assignments for three months to one year in different areas of the company. That way they gain new skills and find out whether they like a new job (or are good at it) before committing to it. "Most staffers return to their original jobs with new knowledge and experiences to share with their workmates, ideally fostering new energy into their collaborations, creativity within their original groups and job satisfaction for themselves," concluded McFarland.

Also, after tracking the pattern of enduring faculty collaborations of newly hired, untenured faculty members over a 15-year period, McFarland found that the enduring ones happen where collaborators find or develop new points of complementarity. "The surviving personal ties are those with a degree of similarity so we can communicate but a degree of difference so we can plumb the relationship for additional value and skills one of us may not yet possess," McFarland says. Ongoing collaboration, mutual mentoring and other kinds of mutual support feel productive and satisfying. Yet periodically seek a new sweet spot of shared interest to keep the relationship thriving like a healthy marriage.

Notice how open and proactive your partner(s) are to seeking renewed complementarity, and around what topics so you can see if they still match your priorities

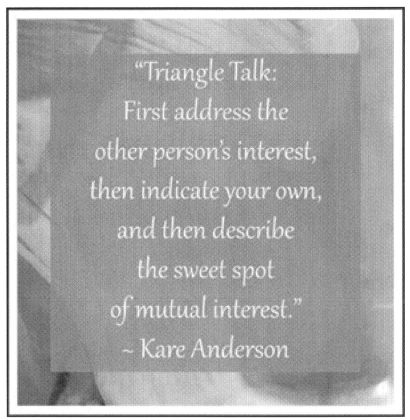

"Triangle Talk:
First address the
other person's interest,
then indicate your own,
and then describe
the sweet spot
of mutual interest."
~ Kare Anderson

As McFarland said, "Cocktail parties encourage people to meet one another and expand their networks, but it takes retreats and team-building exercises to encourage trust, communication, and interdependence among group members. It also requires a willingness to rotate your expertise and roles in relationships, so that you can learn new sides to one another and engage in fresh experiences."

Also, have your organization host both internal-only and also by-invitation events that involve employees or members and potentially complementary individuals from outside the organization. Design some of those events for faster matchups for individuals with shared interests to discover each other.

Use a two-step "lean-then-loose" approach to an event to optimize attendees' chances for making meaningful connections:

Part One, Lean: In a ballroom, host a speed consulting or a speed "find the sweet spot" round table or a "Meet the Pros" roundtable. In the roundtables format, attendees sign up for seats at a table, in two rounds. For the "Sweet Spot" approach, a facilitator at each table guides participants in finding their strongest shared interest. For "Meet the Pros," popularized by the National Speakers Association, each table has an expert who responds to questions.

Part Two, Loose: Host a cocktail hour or buffet meal where participants can mix and mingle to have follow-up discussions with those whose interests they share.

It's Never Too Late to Start a Group That Becomes Close-Knit

Rain or shine for over a decade, my college friend Jane Burns has been walking the same route in Lake Oswego every morning at 7:00 am with the same hardy group of women. Neighbors, yet strangers at first, the habit has bound them together.

Inevitably when the same people meet regularly, they literally get in sync, from pupil dilation to heartbeat. Over time, they talk in shorthand and each truly "gets" what the other is saying, even when they choose silence to convey it. Human walls fall with familiarity.

Over time, repeating a ritual together – especially in motion – boosts instinctive mutuality:

1.   Our regular gatherings become the place where we are most likely to tell the stories that are giving our lives cohesion and meaning.

2.   The gatherings become, over time, an increasingly central part of the narrative of those stories we tell.

"Lots of people want to ride with you in the limo, but what you want is someone who will take the bus with you when the limo breaks down." ~ Oprah Winfrey

Why Start a Closed Group?

When you start a group, you have the opportunity to change the role you play in the stories you tell and live. Change your story and you can change the kind of adventure story you want for your life now.

In this time-starved, often transient world, nothing beats the comfort of a regular ritual of face-to-face contact – especially sharing time in motion – for becoming extremely familiar with each other and increasingly mutually supportive. We women, for example, don't have to be twisted sisters.

Yes, it's helpful to have a previous slight acquaintance, especially as we are making radical changes in our lives or trying on parts of our personalities long forgotten. But with the moves, job and life changes and fewer formal affiliations, we can feel alone when our friends are in different parts of our lives and we do not have a regular group who know us well.

Because we have fewer threads of continuity in our lives, it is well worth the time to create a small group, perhaps around a shared activity, however daunting it might be to suggest such a thing to others. That may be why so many book groups have sprung up – not just to discuss what we've read but how we felt about the book – and our lives.

A client told me he has been part of a group that has gone to movies together, meeting afterwards to dine and talk about what they saw. They just changed to meeting in one person's home, sharing a curved sofa and chairs while watching Netflix-streamed movies on a big screen, and then dining in, potluck style, for a lively discussion about it, learning more – and more deeply – about each other than they might at a traditional dinner party.

Sometimes the best way to start a group is to have a convivial, sharing gathering and see how people gel or not.

"I missed all the girlfriends I left behind and often thought about how a grown woman would ever make friends like that again," she said. "When I started throwing this party, I realized food is one of the best ways to bring people together," said *Cookie Swap* author Julia Usher.

Consider co-hosting your modern version of the cookie exchange or a Sunday potluck. By the way, last December a male friend who'd been working long hours on his biotech start-up wanted to start a regular gathering of friends who were not related to his work. He hosted a cookie exchange with his men friends, suggesting that each bring a favorite they remembered their mother or other family member making and to come with cookies and a related memory to share. All nine showed up.

For an ongoing group, consider two things.

First, settle on a core belief or interest that all potential participants share – your sweet spot of mutual interest that can bind you together.

Second, seek a diverse mix of individuals – not more than seven as that seems to be the limit for becoming close as a group.

"Groups become more extreme and entrenched in their beliefs and polarized from others when members only exchange information that reinforces their views and filter out all else or never learn of alternatives. Thus they narrow their options and magnify each other's prejudices and misconceptions." ~ Cass Sunstein

Your variety of backgrounds means a richer experience together but also the increased potential for misunderstanding or even conflict at times. Yet the opportunity to share and grow exponentially more – emotionally and intellectually – is often worth the effort.

"Everything that irritates us about others can lead us to an understanding of ourselves." ~ Carl Jung

Take a Mutuality Approach to Forming Your Group

If you feel bold enough to recruit one likely member for a small group, tell that person the core interest you'd like all members to share. Ask for feedback and listen closely. That shared interest is the sweet spot and can be group glue. After you find your first person, agree on a total number and together agree on the core interest and the third person to approach. Involve all committed participants in choosing the next prospective member until you have reached your total number of members. Agree on a few rules of engagement on such vital topics as confidentiality, the format for meetings, if any, and let the rest evolve. You are more likely to build trust if you close the group at that number and focus on building the sense of "we" as you get to know and support each other over time.

Hint: Sharing experiences enables us to mirror each other's emotions and thus feel greater empathy for each other. That not only brings us closer, evoking one of the most meaningful memories we can share, looking back on our lives, but it also positively affects the friends of our friend's friends, according to Connected authors James H. Fowler and Nicholas A. Christakis.

Our close-knit group's mutual support ripples out in comforting ways we feel first-hand and in ways we will never know.

As Marco Iacoboni wrote, "Some of us cry when we watch sad movies or wince when we see athletes fall. This sense of shared experience is at the core of human experience. Because our brain has mirror neurons, we are capable of interpreting facial expressions of pain or joy, the first step towards feeling empathy, which causes an instinctively imitative response – the Chameleon Effect." That 'mirroring' response enables two people to literally see they are more alike in that moment. That similarity evokes familiarity and thus a feeling of comfort that can lead to mutual trust. As well, seeing yourself through diverse others' eyes is one of the best ways to identify your strongest talents, maybe even more than using the famous Strengths Finder, suggests Adam Grant. His favorite mirror is called the Reflected Best Self Exercise. Gulp. It involves e-mailing people who know you well, asking them to write a story about a time when you were at your best, and then using the common patterns to create a portrait of your strengths.

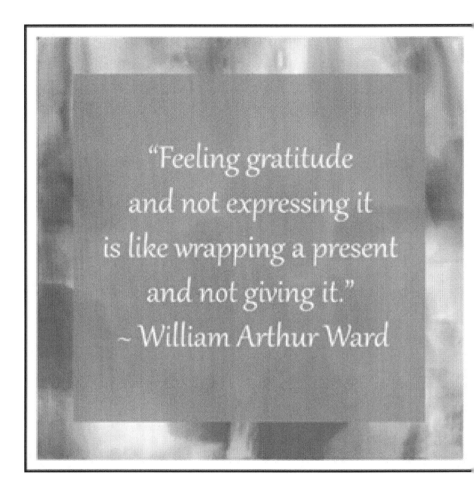

"Feeling gratitude
and not expressing it
is like wrapping a present
and not giving it."
~ William Arthur Ward

Share In Mutually Beneficial Ways
Three Hard-Earned Truths About Helpful Giving

1. Giving That Scales Serendipitous Opportunities

If you give enough people the helpful support they need when they most need it, you often get what *you* most need, when you most need it – sometimes even before you know you need it, and sometimes from those you didn't know could provide it. As former president Bill Clinton said at Maya

Angelou's memorial service, "Nothing is more powerful than those things we share."

2. Giving That Drains Goodwill and Energy

Some individuals give and give and give to you to fulfill their unquenchable need to be known as caring people. Yet what they give is often not relevant to the recipient. One of the most uncomfortable experiences is to have unhelpful help heaped on you by someone who grows increasingly resentful that you aren't returning the favor in equal measure. They are unconscious matchers disguised as givers. Look at your own giving to see if you might inadvertently appear that way to some people.

3. Giving That Supports and Reinforces Our Better Sides

Strengthen others' top talents as you hone yours by being the Opportunity Maker who suggests ways you can use your complementary talents together on a strong sweet spot of mutual interest.

"In everybody's life, at some time, our inner fire goes out. It is then burst into flame by an encounter with another human being. We should all be thankful for those people who rekindle the inner fire."~ Albert Schweitzer

Help Others to Become More Helpful

We can feel that heady, immediate, hedonic high each time we help someone who seeks our advice or an introduction, yet there may be surer ways to support others and ourselves while also spurring them to emulate the giving behavior they experience from you. Those who continue getting the help they ask for, without giving back at all over time, are likely to become takers – *not just with you but also with others.*

Here are models I have experienced that can spur a natural balance and flow of giving and receiving:

Give for the Greater Good of Our Team

The Triangles Game you read about earlier gives visceral proof of the winning power of smartly giving to "our" team for the greater good of all the team. Whenever a team or organizational culture explicitly recognizes and rewards individual giving to the group, individuals seem to become more frequent and adept givers, as in these examples:

• Gore-Tex and Saddleback Church, as I mentioned earlier, are frequently cited as examples of the connective, giving power of small, strong, interconnected teams or groups within a larger organization.

• The specific rules of engagement of how Quantified Self members share self-monitoring experiments in their Meetups has enabled that self-organized group to scale global participation and innovation so rapidly and well that several universities and companies have sought them out as research partners.

• Mutual support communities thrive when they are centered around a strongly felt shared interest. Consider the giving behaviors, for example, in 12-step programs or groups for cancer survivors or avid cyclists. The popularity of these groups and the loyalty members feel to each other and their group illustrate how we will generously give apt advice and help, not seeking a *quid pro quo*, when the shared mission, giving and camaraderie is evident.

• Other kinds of groups with explicit norms and rules to reinforce mutuality of benefits tend to spur greater sharing. They include Mastermind groups of peers and groups led by an expert, such as Vistage groups.

Gain Mastery of Your Talent To Be A Sought-After Ally

In learning anything new we are initially unaware of how little we know. Thus, we are at the bottom of the four-steps of learning, on the ladder to effortless competence created by Noel Burch. Initially, we are unconsciously incompetent at the skill or topic. We don't know what we don't know.

As we learn, we become consciously incompetent and then consciously competent. If we persevere (with grit and tenacity), perhaps taking 10,000 hours as Malcolm Gladwell believes, we eventually develop mastery. We become unconsciously competent when we can get in a flow and perform so well it becomes second nature. At that level you have an extraordinary talent that makes you distinctly valuable for certain situations, especially with other mutuality-minded folks who have mastered complementary talents.

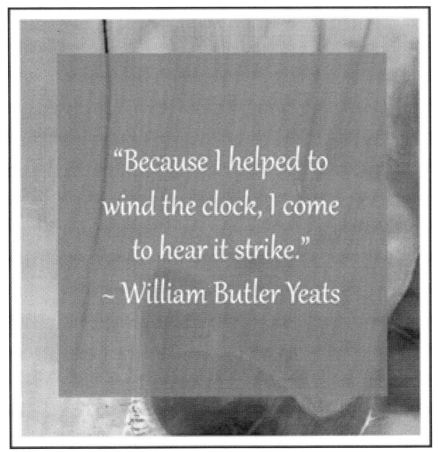

"Because I helped to wind the clock, I come to hear it strike."
~ William Butler Yeats

That's when you can be a helpful giver. Using these four steps toward greater competence, for example, you can help someone know what they don't know or recognize a blind spot. To strengthen this talent, turn to the Johari Window and take a test for greater self-awareness.

While mutuality-minded people don't give to get or keep score on who's giving the most over time, they do recognize a downside in continuing to give to someone who does not. They are sufficiently wise to know that if they keep giving to either matchers or to takers, they are inadvertently reinforcing those two bad habits – both toward them and toward others.

"Action expresses priorities." ~ Mahatma Gandhi

For the joy of giving and to strengthen diverse relationships, here are some efficient and eminently satisfying ways to pay it forward, five or so minutes at a time:

- When sharing what you believe is relevant information or making an introduction, take this extra step with your Five Minute Favor. Ask that person to give candid feedback. Was it helpful? In so doing, you
- Clearly demonstrate that you place a priority on "our" relationship by taking the time.
- Show you want to get ever better at understanding what most matters to that other person.
- Ascertain if that person is willing and trusting enough to be candid back at this stage in your relationship.

Tip: See more ways and times to be helpful givers.

From Marc and Angel, here are 60 more selfless ways and still more from MSN Living, MindBodyGreen, Halfway Point and, of course, Pay it Forward Day.

If you give enough other people what they need, you often find you'll get what *you* need, sometimes before you know you need it, and sometimes from individuals you did not know could provide it.

"Never make someone a priority who only makes you an option." ~ Unknown

Participate in Sharing-Centric Organizations to Grow Friendships, Save Money and Multiply Positive Shared Experiences and Opportunities

If you don't already, probably quite soon you will be saving money – and making money – and meeting kindred spirits by using one or more sharing-based services and/or operating one. Airbnb, for example, is scaling the number of people who can afford to remain in their homes or condos by renting out rooms. Sharing-based systems enable us to buy less stuff, from boats to garments to garden tools, because we can share the use of them. Still others are making a living or moonlighting by operating a sharing-based business. Some of these disruptive, firms, like the on-demand car service Uber are expanded to include boating. Tom Friedman officially declared the sharing economy a trend. Looking at the trends from the perspective of "crowd-powered institutions" and corporations, the Altimeter Group, and others dub the trend theCollaborative Economy, with Jeremiah Owyang citing the threats and opportunities for them.

Sharing-based living and working methods, organizations and experiences will continue to morph, scale and be adopted in more countries and adapted to more situations, causing rippling disruptions to traditional economies as they do.

Look for self-organized, networked local groups that share similar operational structures that speed their capacity to learn from each other and innovate both globally and locally. As mentioned, a great example is Quantified Self, which stays on the forefront of customized personal fitness and healthcare by collectively studying their personal fitness or chronic disease in ways that are sufficiently systematic that university research centers and pharmaceutical firms are recruiting QS groups as partners for faster research results.

Remember the many compartments
of the heart the seed of what is possible.
So much of who we are is defined
by the places we hold for each other.
For it is not our ingenuity
that sets us apart,
but our capacity for love,
the possibility our way will be lit by grace.
Our hearts prisms,
chiseling out the colors of pure light
– Kare Anderson

For your strongest area of expertise, consider adapting that kind of structure to launch a similar, sharing-centric organization. See how they attract and keep avid, high-performing members at QS. First, one seeks a group or individual within QS with the same specific interest, such as wearable health tracking devices, or the same health problem, such as diabetes. Look closely at the underlying Meetup chapter structure and format on which it is based to create your online and in-person model.

Others crowd-attracting models are incentive competitions, like TopCoder, that enable individuals to get well-paid, using their best talents in a transparent, thus purely merit-based way to win that opportunity.

Tip: See what existing organizations and forms of sharing might help you in your work or life. Resources: Neal Gorenflo has been crowdsourcing coverage of such methods at Shareable.net. *On the Commons* magazine covers collaborative ways of working and published *All That We Share*.

Roo Rogers and Rachel Botsman, co-authors of *What's Mine is Yours*, continue curating examples of *Collaborative Consumption*, including a directory of them. In her book *Mesh* and her TED talk, Lisa Gansky describes how businesses can be built to "provide people with goods and services at the exact moment they need them, without the burden and expense of owning them outright." See her directory and global gathering.

Craft Sharing Methods That Are Immediately Useful

The more specific and immediately useful the idea, the more "spreadable" it becomes. Usually the most successful community-building methods are based on efficient ways to be mutually supportive and accountable.

Own Less. Share More. Get Closer.

From locally sharing things you no longer need, via Freecycle or seldom use, co-working spaces and shared business places and co-promotion, to aging in place among tight-knit neighbors via variations of The Village Movement, started in Beacon Hill, that enables us to age in place among tight-knit neighbors with apt experts and tools, the good news is that sharing methods are morphing and spreading. When people do discover concrete ways they can be mutually supportive, they tend to adopt them and then modify them and tell others. Word naturally spreads.

Tip: When people collaborate around an explicit shared interest, they tend to bring out the better sides in each other so they inevitably get closer and accomplish more. That spiral up into mutually reinforcing support.

Conversely, when a sharing system does not have a strong sweet spot of shared interest and methods of mutual support, the community can spiral down into competition and conflict.

We End This Book, Circling Around to Where We Began

Ready to turn the page now, to the adventure story you are truly meant to live with others? You are more likely to move into a mutuality mindset if you do these things within the next 24 hours:

1.   Look deeply inward to recognize your strongest moments when you are most happy and appreciated – doing what with whom. What specific activities and what complementary traits in others are the biggest magnifiers of your talents and satisfaction – and theirs?

2.   Ask one of the individuals who comes most strongly to mind, in light of that contemplation, to get together this week to explore the potential sweet spot of shared interest you saw in your thoughts. When you meet: Speak warmly and specifically. Listen closely. Respond directly. Talk iteratively. Who knows? Together you may find an even sweeter sweet spot of mutual interest.

3.   All mutuality minded relationships don't have to be productive, just mutually satisfying – in love, friendship, work, or cause support. Yet, ironically, when you click with one or more others in mutuality, it inevitably results in something

productive. I'm sure you won't be disappointed to discover how often that is true.

I'm counting on you to share with others, including me, some of the stumbles and successes as you practice proving, in your own uniquely remarkable way, that mutuality matters in making lives better for us and others. Of course, some of the people whose lives you will affect in this way may never become known to you. Yet the rippling effects of your beneficial actions – *with others* – may inspire a shift in just a few people away from the slippery slope of treachery toward others.

"It's not about what you build, but what others build off of what you've built." ~ Tim Berners-Lee

Because Dan Ariely and other researchers foresee, in our increasingly virtual world, a greater temptation and opportunity to cheat, your actions in support of the opposite direction are ever more vital in our world now. Yes, I was saving this final grim nudge to give you one last reason to move toward mutuality. Addressing your better side, I believe it worked.

Be Quoted In The Next Edition Of This Book?

Perhaps I can feature one or more of your favorite, actionable mutuality tips and a related example – or one you've learned from someone else and properly attribute to them. Send me your specific method and example for becoming more mutuality minded: kare@sayitbetter.com Thank you.

"Share the story
in which others see a role
they want to play
so they may re-shape it
and share it."
~ Kare Anderson

"Let's be greater together."
~ Kare Anderson

Please send them to me at kare@sayitbetter.com, in 200 words or less, with links, your full name, e-mail address and your main URL. Together we can help others, and perhaps enjoy a flourishing friendship.

Thank you! ~ Kare Anderson

You can start and strengthen mutuality-centric relationships with those you value by socially sharing 140 potential "Aha moments" from this book that most resonate with you.

Here's how. Get my free companion book to Mutuality Matters, filled with 140 Twitter-sized quotes, produced by THiNKaha® for the Aha Amplifier™.

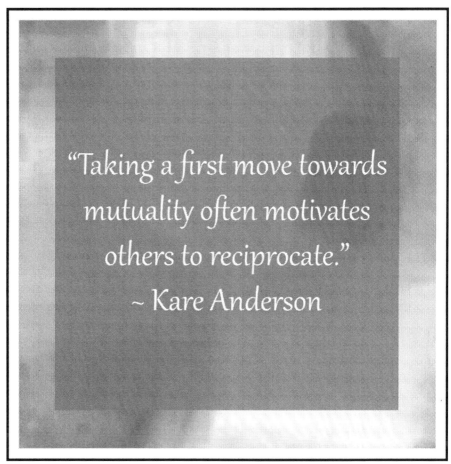

"Taking a first move towards mutuality often motivates others to reciprocate."
~ Kare Anderson

You can share them on Twitter, Facebook, LinkedIn and Google+.

Steps:

1. Click on http://bit.ly/KareAnderson-Aha01 to create a free Aha Amplifier account simply by verifying your email address.

2. Click on my book, scroll to the bottom and click on the button to download my book for free.

3. Share quotes by clicking on a button from the "Activate" tab.

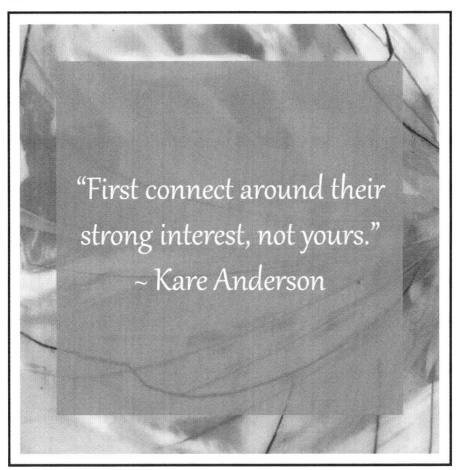

"First connect around their strong interest, not yours."
~ Kare Anderson

52 Tips For Weekly Practice: Move Through Your Year Into Deeper Mutuality

1. It is never too late to turn the page to a new chapter of the adventure story you are truly meant to live *with others*

2. Whatever most captures your mind controls your life. Let a Mutuality Mindset become top-of-mind

3. Spending time with those you respect bolsters, in you, the traits you most admire in them.

4. The better you know your best talent & temperament the more adept you become in finding those with complementary traits

5. Interconnectedness increases frequency of serendipitous encounters & unexpected insights that enable faster innovation

6. Strangers can be consequential when you want to practice an atrophied or unexplored facet of you, as they don't know how you usually act

7. Becoming more deeply connected with those you admire and love bolsters, in you, the traits you most admire in them.

8. Consistently remind yourself why you appreciate your closest, most mutuality-centric allies to guard against taking them for granted.

9. Label yourself before someone else does so you are a distinctive, discoverable ally for apt acts of mutual support.

10. Recognize behaviors that most upset you so, like defensive driving, you can see potential "crashes" sooner and avoid them

11. Speak sooner to a sweet spot of shared interest to cultivate a meaningful connection, the first step to creating something greater together.

12. Triangle Talk: Cite 1. Their interest 2. How your interest cooincides with it 3. Action we could take.

13. Share the story in which others see a role they want to playso they will re-shape it, share it and make it "our" story

14. Boost understanding, competence & connection: keep messages, rules & requests simple & brief

15. Create a clear explanation? Ask an expert & novice to craft it: Expert knows too much (curse of knowledge) & novice sees it with fresh eyes

16. Whoever most vividly characterizes a situation usually determines how others see it, talk about it, and make decisions about it.

17. Demonstrate warmth first, then competence, not the reverse. We're highly sensitive to warmth and its absence.

18. Before meeting or re-meeting someone, think of what youmost like and admire about that person + keep it top-of-mind as you meet.

19. We tend to like each other better when walking, sitting or standing side by side or at right angles from each other.

20. Bring out the better side in others and they are more likely to see and support yours.

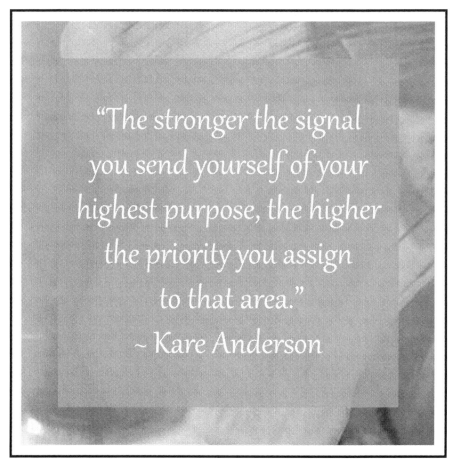

"The stronger the signal you send yourself of your highest purpose, the higher the priority you assign to that area."
~ Kare Anderson

21. Speak to their positive intent especially when it appears they have none, and you are more like to see it appear.

22. Magnify the power of your praise by making it visible, in-person and virtually, especially to those who most matter to people whom you praise.

23. When the spotlight's on you, shine it on those you admire, citing their positive exploits, thus making it brighter for them & you

24. Adopt the *Golden* Golden Rule. Do unto others as they would have done unto them.

25. Praise the behaviors in others that you most want to flourish.

26. Identify a noble shared purpose as the context in which you work with others.

27. A large, diverse group of non-experts often outperforms a small group of experts

28. Inclusion inspires innovation because we see more sides of situations.

29. Accomplish more. Seek opposites: pessimists/optimists, fast/slow thinkers, maintainers/creators, introverts/extroverts

30. Accomplishing one thing greater together is the strongest spur to work on something even bigger next time.

31. Don't just be a giver. Be an extremely helpful giver who demonstrates an awareness of what they most need.

32. Give enough others what they need & U often get what U need, sometimes before U know U need it & from those U didn't know could provide it

33. Sharing experiences enables us to mirror each other's emotions and thus feel greater empathy for each other.

34. Few things attract as much attention & credibility as 3 unlikely allies, ardently united around something

35. In the midst of a mess, who is thriving and how can we help others thrive like them?

36. When you see someone's interest rise in the conversation, ask follow-up questions, to get closer to their sweet spot of strong interest.

37. Take notes. It demonstrates interest & respect and moves you towards mutuality

38. Set regular times for cross-functional, candid and facilitated discussions of projects

39. Make it easier, faster or more fun for us to do the right thing for each other, plus enable us to feel proud when we do

40. Self-Fulfilling Prophecy Effect: When first meeting, ask each teammate to give a reason they look forward to working together.

41. To create *close-knit teams* never have more than seven members – with no extra members – and agree on a top goal & rules of engagement.

42. We are high performing and happier in large organizations when working in small, tight-knit teams that regularly interact with other teams.

43. Do not make someone else a priority when they only make you an option. Actions show real priorities.

44. Respond to insults as opportunities to show visible kindness, thus spurring observers to do the same & become unified with you.

45. As a connective leader, demonstrating that being a strong team player is as important as being a rising star.

46. Bright spots: Find the things we're doing right, and figure out how to do them more often.

47. Make your expression a welcoming gift: avoid the dour "screen face" from staring down at your phone.

48. Does your project or business have a "hook" on which others can proudly and *visibly contribute*? #MutualityMatters

49. Co-create a ritual and/or object that reinforces our mutuality such as a hand signal, slogan, or image.

50. In a civilization when love is gone we turn to justice and when justice is gone we turn to power and when power is gone we turn to violence.

51. We can't know which interactions will deepen into richer relationships, yet we can keep the faith that our mutuality mindset affirms them.

52. Mutuality most demonstrates our humanity and, in the end, that may be what most matters.

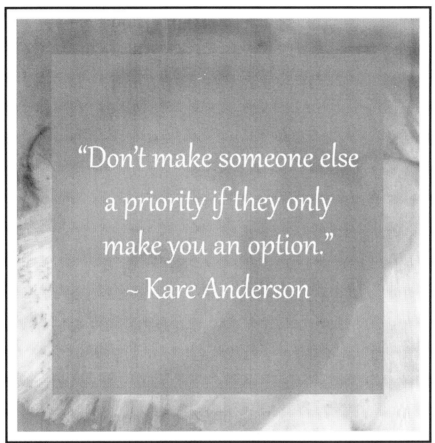

"Don't make someone else a priority if they only make you an option."
~ Kare Anderson

AllTop is a Guy Kawasaki co-founded site where the most popular blog posts in each category, such as collaboration orcoworking, gain the most visibility, thus spurring contributors to an ever higher bar of excellence in our area of expertise. We are also quickly able to quickly see some of the best ideas and thought leaders in the sectors we seek to serve.

Adam Alter
@AdamLeeAlter
Alter is the author of Drunk Tank Pink, and a professor of marketing and psychology at New York University.

John Baldoni
@JohnBaldoni
Baldoni is the author of 12 books including Lead with Purpose, and Moxie, and chairman of the leadership development practice at N2Growth.

Albert-Laszlo Barabasi
Barabasi is the author of Linked and Bursts, and a pioneer in real-world network theory.

Melinda Blau
@MelindaBlau
Blau is the co-author, along with Karen Fingerman, of Consequential Strangers and other books.

Bob Burg
@BobBurb
Burg is the co-author, along with John David Mann, of The Go-Giver and author of Adversaries into Allies and other books.

David Berreby

@davidberreby
Berreby is author of Us and Them and the blog, Mind Matters.

Rachel Botsman
@rachelbotsman
Botsman is co-author, along with Roo Rogers, of What's Mine is Yours, and founder of Collaborative Lab which helps governments and companies benefit from the collaborative economy.

Ori Brafman and Rom Brafman
@Oribrafman
Ori and Rom Brafman are the co-authors of Sway and The Starfish and the Spider.

Greg Brandeau
@Brandeau
Brandeau is co-author, with Linda Hill, Kent Lineback and Emily Truelove of Collective Genius, and president of Maker Media.

Bob Burg
@BobBurg
Burg is the author of *Go-Giver* and *Adversaries into Allies*.

John Cacioppo
@J_Cacioppo @ccsn_uchicago
Cacioppo is the author of Loneliness, University of Chicago professor and director of the Center for Cognitive and Social Neuroscience.

Susan Cain
@susancain
Cain is the author of Quiet.

Nicholas Christakis
@NAChristakis
Christakis is the co-author, along with James Fowler, of Connected, and a professor at Yale University, working at the boundary of the natural and social sciences.

Robert Cialdini
@RobertCialdini
Cialdini is the author of Influence.

Tyler Cohen
@tylercowen
Cohen is co-author, with Alex Tabarrok, of the behavioral economic blog, Marginal Revolution, and a professor of economics at George Mason University.

Cohousing Movement
@cohousing
Cohousing specializes in fostering intentional neighborhoods, and private homes with shared areas and common meals.

Collaborative Housing
@CollabHousing
Collaborative Housing advocates urban development that combines private and shared residential spaces with commercial spaces.

Co-operative News
@coopnews
Co-operative News champions the global co-operative movement.

Common Spark
@CommonSpark

Common Spark is a collective that's building a collection of commons maps and threat maps: the Commons Atlas.

Lauren Cucinotta
@LCucinotta
Cucinotta is the head of community engagement for TEDx at TED conferences.

Amy Cuddy
@amyjccuddy
Cuddy is a social psychologist who uses experimental methods to investigate how people judge and influence each other and themselves.

Roger Dooley
@rogerdooley
Dooley is the author of Braininfluence and publisher of Neuromarketing where brain science and marketing meet.

James R. Doty, M.D.
@StanfordCCARE
Doty is a clinical professor of neurosurgery, Huffington Post blogger, and founder and director of The Center for Compassion and Altruism Research and Education at Stanford University.

Robin Dreeke
@Dreeke
Dreeke is the author of It's Not All about "Me", founder of People Formula, lead instructor at the FBI's Counterintelligence Training Center in all behavioral and interpersonal skills training, and lead instructor at the FBI's Counterintelligence Training Center in all behavioral and interpersonal skills training.

Kevin Dutton
@profkevindutton
Dutton is the author of *The Wisdom of Psychopaths*, *Flipnosis* and, with Andy McNab, Good Psychopath's Guide to Success; and a research psychologist at the University of Oxford.

Paul Ekman
@PaulEkman
Ekman is the author of Moving Toward Compassion, Telling Lies and Emotions Revealed, and a pioneering expert on reading faces.

Nicholas Epley
Epley is the author of Mindwise and director of Self and Social Judgment Laboratory at the University of Chicago,

eRepublic
@eRepublic
eRepublic provides smart media approaches for public sector innovation, especially for state and local government and education.

Nir Eyal
@nireyal
Eyal is the author of Hooked and writes about the intersection of psychology and business.

Tom Farsides
@TomFarsides
Farsides studies and writes about altruism, and prosocial behavior.

Carlin Flora
@carlinf

Flora *is the author* of Friendfluence, and former editor at Psychology Today.

Chad Forbes
@ChadForbes
Forbes is a professor of social neuroscience who studies the consequences of stereotyping on brain and behavior.

Jon Freeman
@freemanjb @freemanlab
Freeman is the director of the Social Cognitive and Neural Sciences Lab at Dartmouth.

Stew Friedman
@StewFriedman @BizRadio111
Friedman is the author of Total Leadership and Baby Bust, and a management professor at Wharton, director of the Work/Life Integration Project, and host of Work and Life radio program.

James H. Fowler
@James_H_Fowler
Fowler is the co-author of Connected, and a professor at UCSD, dedicated to the intersection of the natural and social sciences.

Joshua Freedman
@eqjosh
Freedman is the leader of the Emotional Intelligence Network.

Todd Gailun
@ToddGailun @TEDxLowerEastSide.

Gailun is co-CEO of Sensoka, a platform for measuring and contextualizing human emotion via wearable devices.

GEO Collective
@GEO_Collective
GEO Collective catalyzes worker co-ops.

John Gerzema
@johngerzema
Gerzema is co-author, along with Michael D'Antonio, of Athena Doctrine, an expert in the use of data to identify social change, a fellow at the Athena Center on Leadership at Barnard, and advocate for U.N. Girl Up Campaign.

Judith E. Glaser
@CreatingWE
Glaser is the author of Creating WE, Conversational Intelligence and four other books, and chairman of The Creating WE Institute.

Daniel Goleman
@DanielGolemanEI
Goleman is the author of Emotional Intelligence who also researches and writes about social intelligence and ecological intelligence.

Sam Gosling
@SamGoslingPsych
Gosling is the author of Snoop and social psychologist at University of Texas at Austin.

Gottman Institute
@GottmanIst

Gottman Institute offers tools, training and books to strengthen relationships, based on 40 years of research.

Mark Goulston, M.D.
@MarkGoulston
Goulston is author Just Listen and co-founder of Heartfelt Leadership.

Adam Grant
@AdamMGrant
Grant is the author of Give and Take, and business professor at Wharton.

Charles H. Green
@CharlesHGreen
Green is the author of Trusted Advisor Fieldbook and co-author of Trust-Based Selling.

Joseph Grenny
@josephgrenny
Grenny is a co-author, along with Kerry Patterson, Ron McMillan and Al Switzler of Crucial Conversations, Crucial Accountability, Influencer, and Change Anything, and a social scientist.

Steven Handel
@StevenHandel
Handel, at The Emotion Machine, writes about psychology and self Improvement: understanding intersections between our thoughts, emotions, habits, relationships, health, and culture.

Pelle G. Hansen
@Peguha
Hansen is a behavioral researcher, and chair of the Danish Nudging Network.

Scott Heiferman
@heif
Heiferman is CEO of Meetup.

Dr. Susan Heitler
@DrSusanHeitler
Heitler is co-author with Paula Singer, of the Power of Two, psychologist, columnist and family therapist.

David Horsager
@DavidHorsager
Horsager is the author of The Trust Edge.

Humor Research Lab
@HumorCode @PeterMcGraw
This University of Colorado lab is led by 'The Humor Code' co-author Peter McGraw.

Michael Hyatt
@Michael Hyatt
Hyatt is the author of Platform, and blogger on intentional leadership.

Marco Iacoboni
@marcoiacoboni
Iacoboni is the author of Mirroring People and a UCLA neuroscientist.

Ideas 42
@ideas42
Ideas 42 is a design and research lab that uses behavioral economics to address complex social problems.

Rana el Kaliouby
@kaliouby @Affectiva

Kaliouby is co-founder and chief science officer at Affectiva and former research scientist at MIT Media Lab, making emotion-enabled interactions and analytics ubiquitous.

Dave Kerpen
@DaveKerpen @LikeableLocal @LikeableMedia @LikeableBook.
Kerpen is the author of *Likeable Business*, *Likeable Social Media* and other likeable books.

Gary Klein
@Kleinsight
Klein is the author of Seeing What Others Don't, The Power of Intuition, and Sources of Power, and a senior scientist atMacroCognition.

Matthew Kohut
@besmonte @CompellingPeeps
Kohut is co-author, with John Neffinger, of 'Compelling People' and co-founder of KNP Communications.

Maria Konnikova
@mkonnikova @newyorker
Konnikova is the author of Mastermind, and The Confidence Game, and a writer for The New Yorker.

Bryan Kramer
@BryanKramer @PureMatter
Kramer is the author of There is no B2B or B2C, and ceo of global digital agency, Pure Matter.

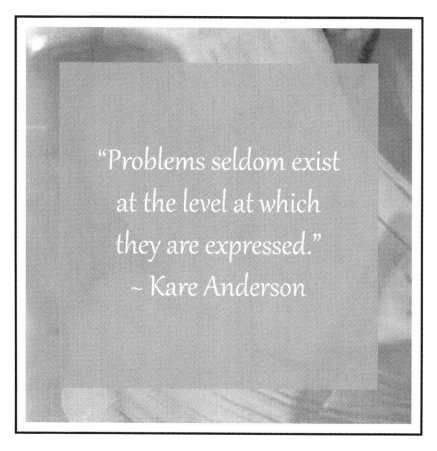

"Problems seldom exist at the level at which they are expressed."
~ Kare Anderson

Jonah Lehrer
@jonahlehrer
Lehrer is the author of *Imagine, How We Decide, Proust Was a Neuroscientist* and other books, who has returned to writing after plagiarism charges.

Harriet Lerner
@HarrietLerner
Lerner is the author of Marriage Rules and The Dance of Anger.

Matt Lieberman
@social_brains
Lieberman is the author of Social and a UCLA neuroscientist.

Thalma Lobel

Lobel is the author of Sensation, psychologist and a professor at the School of Psychological Science at Tel Aviv University where she is director of the child development center, and Huffington Post blogger.

Dave Logan
@davelogan1 @tribaleadership @CultureSync
Logan is the co-author, with John King, of Tribal Leadership, and University of Southern California professor.

Glenn Llopis
@GlennLlopis
Llopis is the author of Earning Serendipity, and a contributor to Forbes, Harvard Business Review and Huffington Post.

Marsha Lucas
@DrMarsha
Lucas is the author of Rewire Your Brain For Love, and a psychologist, and neuropsychologist.

Maker's Nation
@MakersNation @ibwatson
Maker's Nation is a network of creative entrepreneurs who support each other.

Deepak Malhotra
@Prof_Malhotra
Malhotra is the author of Negotiation Genius and I Moved Your Cheese, and professor at Harvard Business School.

Gary Marcus
@GaryMarcus

Marcus is the author of Guitar Zero, Kluge, and The Birth of the Brain, and research psychologist focuses on language, biology and the mind, and blogger for The New Yorker.

Benita Matofska
@benitamatofska @compareandshare @peoplewhoshare
Matofska is the chief sharer at Compare and Share, the world's first comparision marketplace.

Massimo Menichinelli
@openp2pdesign
Menichinelli leads metadesign projects for open systems that enable collaborative projects.

Nilofer Merchant
@nilofer @Thinkers50
Merchant is the author of the 11 Rules for Creating Value in the Social Era, and a writer for Harvard Business Review.

Kelly McGonigal
@kellymcgonigal
McGonigal is the author of The Willpower Instinct, TED presenter, and a psychologist.

Meshing
@sharethemesh
The Mesh is a global community, led by The Mesh author Lisa Gansky, serving the sharing economy.

Jerry Michalski
@jerrymichalski

Michalski is founder of REX, a consultancy that helps companies navigate the Relationships Economy Xpedition.

Katherine Milkman
@katy_milkman @Wharton
Milkman is an assistant professor of behavioral economist at Wharton who studies, judgment, and decisionmaking, with an interest in human limitations and how to overcome them

Richard Millington
@RichMillington
Millington is the author of Buzzing Communities, an expert at online communities, and managing director of FeverBee.

Gaurav Mishra
@Gauravonomics
Mishra is a writer, speaker and trainer using emerging technologies to create communities, crowdsource actions and change behaviors.

MIT Mood Meter
@MITMoodMeter
MIT Mood Meter assessed the overall mood of MIT by using facial recognition software in cameras at four locations to determine the number of smiles.

Sylvia Morelli
@SylviaMorelli
Morelli is a postdoctoral Fellow at Stanford Social Neuroscience Lab studying neural and behavioral basis of empathy, feeling understood and perspective-taking.

Jonathan Moreno

@pennprof
Moreno is the author of The Body Politic, Mind Wars, and other books, and a medical ethics and health policy professor at University of Pennsylvania whose online neuroethics course drew more than 36,000 registrants in 2013.

Michael Myatt
@MikeMyatt
Myatt is the author of Hacking Leadership, and Leadership Matters, and chairman at N2Growth.

Oui Share
@OuiShare @OuiShare_fr
Oui Share is a global network empowering citizens, public institutions and companies to build a collaborative society

Jeremiah Owyang
@jowyang
Owyang is the founder of Crowd Companies where corporations partner in the collaborative economy.

Eli Pariser
@elipariser @Upworthy
Pariser is the author of The Filter Bubble, and co-founder of Upworthy.

Peers
@peers
Peers is a member-driven organization to support the sharing economy movement.

Alex Pentland
@alex_pentland

Pentland is the author of Social Physics and Honest Signals, and professor at MIT.

Gianpiero Petriglieri
@gpetriglieri @insead
Petriglieri is a professor of organizational behavior at INSEAD, psychiatrist, and writer leadership, identity, meaning and daily life.

Steven Pinker
@sapinker
Pinker is author of *The Sense of Style*, *The Better Angels of our Nature* and other books, and a cognitive scientist at Harvard.

Margarita Quihuis
@msquihuis
Quihuis is the co-author of The Pax Urbana, and co-director of the Peace Innovation Lab, which is part of Stanford Persuasive Technology Lab.

Ashwin Ram
@ashwinram @PARCinc @OpenStudy @GeorgiaTech
Ram is the chief innovation officer of interactive intelligence at PARC, an expert in augmented social cognition, and co-founder at Open Study.

Jessica Remedios
@jdremedios
Remedios is a psychology professor at Tufts, studying stereotyping, prejudice, stigma, and identity.

Jonathan Rowson
@Jonathan_Rowson @theRSAorg
Rowson is the director of the Social Brain Centre.

Daniel Simons
@ProfSimons @cfchabris
Simons is co-author, with Christopher Chabris, of The Invisible Gorilla, and cognitive psychology professor at the University of Illinois.

Shareable
@Shareable
Shareable covers news and ideas for sharable practices and nonprofits.

Shareable City
@shareable_city @urbanohumano
Shareable City provides ways for residents to efficiently and safely share and creating more connected communities.

Simon Sinek
@simonsinek
Sinek is author of Leaders Eat Last and Start With Why, and a contributor to Huffington Post, BrandWeek and Harvard Business Review.

The Social Science Research Council
@SSRC_org
SSRC is an independent, non-profit research organization that uses social science research to address critical social issues.
http://www.ssrc.org

Social Science Research Network
@SSRN
SSRN supports is the rapid worldwide dissemination of social science research and is composed of a number of specialized research networks in each of the social sciences.

Leah Somerville

@leahsom

Somerville is an assistant professor of psychology, director of the Affective Neuroscience and Development Lab at Harvard University, and a fan of science and sarcasm.

Stanford Leadership

@StnfrdLeadrship

The Leadership Initiative at Stanford supports a community of scholars, students, and practitioners to develop principled, world-changing leaders.

StirToAction

@StirToAction

Stir to Action is a quarterly print magazine of community-based, cooperative and commons alternatives.

http://stirtoaction.com/pre-order-winter-issue-25-off/

Maia Szalavitz

@maiasz

Szalavitz is the author of Born for Love, and neuroscience journalist at TIME.com.

ServiceSpace

@servicespace

Service Space supports ten generosity-driven projects involving over 341,000 members. Member organizations include DailyGood, KarmaTube and PledgePage.

Laura Stein

@citizenstein

Stein is the founder of TEDx.

Don Tapscott
@dtapscott
Tapscott is
the author of *Macrowikinomics*, *Wikinomics*, *Growing Up Digital*, and *Macrowikinomics*, and executive director ofGlobal Solutions Networks.

Richard H. Thaler
@R_Thaler
Thaler is co-author with Cass Sunstein of Nudge, and professor of behavioral science and economics at the University of Chicago.

Judith C. Tingley
@drtingley
Tingley is the author of books for women: *Say What You Mean. Get What You Want*, *Genderflex*, *GenderSell*, *The Power of Indirect Influence*, and *Break the Negative Self-Talk Habit*.

TriplePundit.com
@triplepundit
Triple Pundit is an online publication that covers CSR, social entrepreneurship, green jobs, and the triple bottom line in sustainable business.

Jay Van Bavel
@jayvanbavel
Van Bavel is a social psychology professor at New York University, studying the flexibility of social, moral and political cognition.

Ben Waber
@bwaber @sociometric @medialab @peopleanalytics

Waber is the author of People Analytics, president and CEO of Sociometric and Media Lab, and a former senior researcher at Harvard Business School.

Jay Walljasper
@JayWalljasper
Walljasper is editor of OnTheCommons.org, columnist at Shareable.net, a fellow at Project for Public Spaces, a senior associate at Citiscope, and a fellow at Augsburg College.

Liz Wiseman
@LizWiseman
Wiseman is the author of The Multiplier Effect and Multipliers, and a leadership educator.

Philip Zimbardo
@PhilZimbardo @HIPorg
Zimbardo is co-author, with John Boyd, of The Time Paradox, and the author of The Lucifer Effect and other books. He led the Stanford Prison Experiment, is research psychologist, and an expert on the origins of evil, who now heads the Heroic Imagination Project.

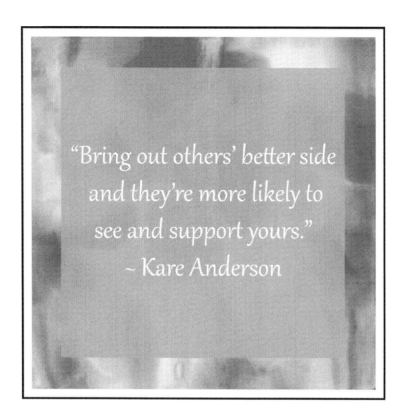

"Bring out others' better side
and they're more likely to
see and support yours."
~ Kare Anderson

About the Author, Kare Anderson

A daydreamer, once labeled "phobically shy" by a school counselor (I snuck into her desk to find her analysis) I am deeply grateful for how these setbacks set me on a path towards mutuality. I've discovered a humanity-affirming secret. When we know how to cultivate an "us" attitude in connecting with others, we can open our lives to considerable more adventure, accomplishment and meaning.

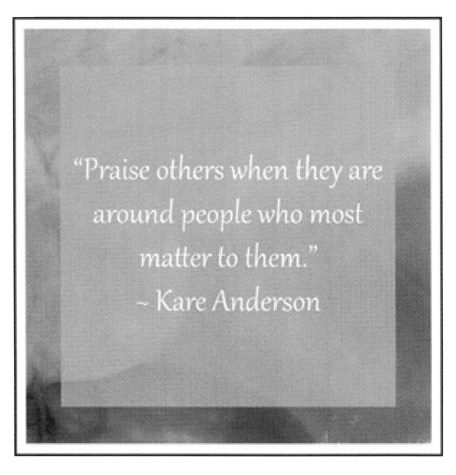

"Praise others when they are around people who most matter to them."
~ Kare Anderson

A mutuality mindset magnifies and multiplies opportunities. Without honing that approach I would never have been able to become an Emmy-winning NBC commentator or reporter for the *Wall Street* Journal? Or co-founded nine women's political action committees? Or been able to speak around the world, and to coach individuals as diverse as surgeons, pro athletes, CFOs? Each experience led to increasingly diverse, mutuality-centric friendships. Speaking at a TED IBM and TEDx Berkeley on mutuality is a natural extension of my writing and speaking on how to become more deeply connected and widely quoted.

I am a public speaker, and a contributor at Forbes and Huffington Post. Also I am the author of Moving From Me to We, *Getting What You Want, Walk Your*

Talk and *Resolving Conflict Sooner*. I was a founding board member of Annie's Homegrown and am a current member of several boards including Raynforest, TEDx Marin, Watermark, and Gloopt.

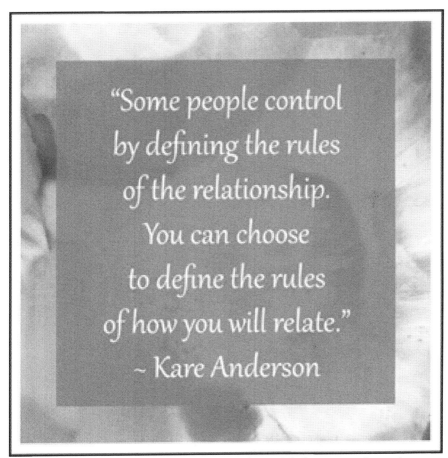

"Some people control by defining the rules of the relationship. You can choose to define the rules of how you will relate."
~ Kare Anderson

Next I'll be writing on how to be widely quoted, perhaps citing you. Here's to our supporting each other in cultivating a mutuality, strong ground on which to become more connective communicators, in what we say and do with others, eh?

About The Artist, Rebecca L. Shapiro

Rebecca Shapiro is that rare mix of fine artist, illustrator, and adept organizer of special interest organizations and communities ranging from TEDxMtHood to Freelancers Union and Ladies Who Launch. One of her key talents is helping individuals reimagine and reconfigure their organizations to grow faster.

A creator, long before she even knew the word "artist," Rebecca's art is as diverse as an interactive installation at the Portland International Airport to encaustic paintings, and photographs and illustrations for distillery and organic food industries. She sees her art as a gateway to a common place for us to meet, and to share our similar stories, struggles and triumphs. Shapiro strives to make art that is both a metaphor and a catalyst for creating stronger relationships and communities. In this way, her art becomes a universal connector, offering us opportunities to deepen awareness, discover fresh ideas, and gain unexpected insights from each other and from our surroundings.

"Strengths spread just as fears do. Supplant your fear with a greater motivation."
~ Kare Anderson

A freelancer for most of her adult life, she can count on one hand the number of full time jobs she's held. Since Shapiro was an eight-year-old babysitter, she's earning her own money. She has launched and owned multiple micro-businesses. Along the way Rebecca gotten valuable skills, life lessons and personal growth. She's gained first-hand experience about the struggles, process, grit, and vision it takes to be a freelancer, as she's described in her book, *Work Independently & Live Connectedly: 52 Steps to Freelancing Freedom.*

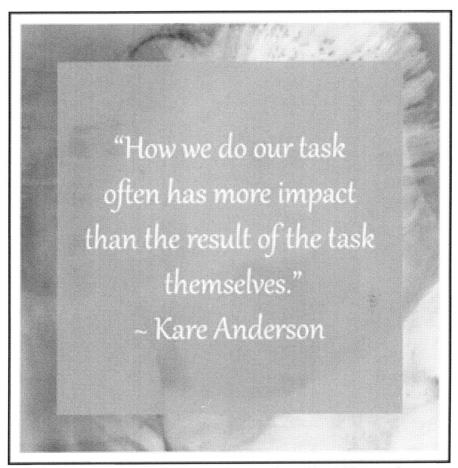

"How we do our task often has more impact than the result of the task themselves."
~ Kare Anderson

Shapiro learned graphic design and medical illustration at the University of Texas Medical School (Houston) then went on to study with noted photographer Carl Chiarenza and printmaker Dwight Pogue while earning aBA in Studio Art from Smith College. She studied photography and printmaking at the Glassell School of Art,Museum of Fine Arts, Houston, and was a five-time recipient of the Frank Freed Memorial Scholarship for Printmaking. She also studied with figurative abstractionist, Ted Katz, in Portland, Oregon. As well, Shapiro is the local Portland organizer for Freelancers Union and works with TEDxMtHood (formerly TEDxConcordiaUPortland) over the past two years to create a robust Artist-in-Residence Program. They are now taking the Artist-in-Residence Program to the world. TED selected the program to be one of twoincubator programs for TEDx organizations that want to create their own Artist-in-Residence program.

About the book designer, formatter & web guru

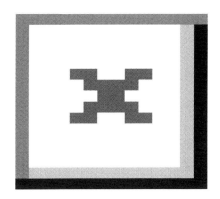

David LaFontaine

David bills himself as a "Creative Data Scientist," because he believes that there is a glaring need for people who can operate both in the world of arts & design – and in numbers, statistics, and bottom-line business imperatives. He has worked as a researcher and designer, content strategist, and trainer for a variety of clients, including: The Herman Ostrow School of Dentistry, U.S. State Department, Pluralsight, KelbyOne Media, Wiley Publishing, B3Communications, AssetShield, and Roundabout Entertainment.

David has written or coauthored five books, including *Social Media Design For Dummies*, *Mobile Web Design For Dummies*, and *Poison Pen*. He has also produced more than 20 hours of online training videos for KelbyOne and Pluralsight.

David has taught Digital Immersion, Online Multimedia, and Digital Publishing at the Annenberg School for Journalism at the University of Southern California. He has also lectured at universities around the world, including at the Institute for the Digital Future of Journalism at the Mohyla University in Kiev, Ukraine; the Nelson Mandala School of Journalism in Addis Ababa, Ethiopia; and at the University Mayor in Santiago, Chile.

In 2012, he traveled to Ethiopia as a Fulbright Specialist for 6 weeks to train NGOs, journalists, and pro-democracy groups in digital media skills.

David started his career as a journalist with a Pulliam Fellowship and worked as a copy editor at the Arizona Republic. From there, he went to Venezuela to work as the managing editor of the Caracas Daily Journal (now the Latin American Herald-Tribune).

You can find out more about Dave on his personal site, http://davidlafontaine.com, or by visiting his blog at http://sipsfromthefirehose.com. He lives in Los Angeles, works in cyberspace, and his curiosity and willingness to use himself as a human lab rat help him keep up with technology trends, test the latest digital tools, and develop a wide range of design and development skills.

Keep It Real: Real Advice for Real World
by Lori Ruff

"The more you feel the rightness of your thoughts, ideas and words; and the more they resonate with the people you speak to, the more boldly you will speak the truths that you see. You might not always feel right, but your words will resonate with people in a way you've never before experienced."

Mental Toughness for Women Leaders: 52 Tips to Recognize and Utilize Your Greatest Strengths
by LaRae Quy

"Strength doesn't come from what you can do. It comes from overcoming the things you once thought you couldn't do. Mental toughness is believing you believe you can prevail in your circumstances rather than believing your circumstances will change."

Work Independently & Live Connectedly: 52 Steps To Freelancing Freedom
by Rebecca L. Shapiro

"Successful freelancers savor their work because they have discovered how to work independently and live connectedly. They cultivate generous, reciprocal relationships that enable them to use their best talents with others."

"Creating mutuality with unexpected allies leads to greater accomplishments and a more meaningful life."

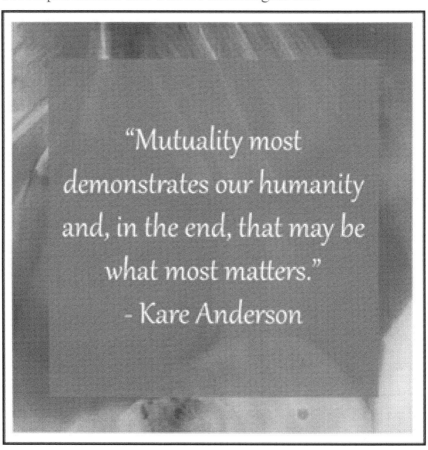

"Mutuality most demonstrates our humanity and, in the end, that may be what most matters."
- Kare Anderson

Manufactured by Amazon.ca
Bolton, ON

15221223R00111